# Arrah-na-Pogue

**Dionysius Lardner Boursiquot,** commonly known as Dion Boucicault, 'the most conspicuous English dramatist of the 19th century' (*New York Times*), was a witty, selfish and deceitful charmer, a bigamist, a profligate spendthrift and the author of dozens of successful plays, only a handful of which endure. Among these his early comedies influenced Oscar Wilde, and his Irish melodramas Shaw, Synge and O'Casey.

**Scott Boltwood** is an Associate Professor of English at Emory and Henry College, Virginia. He has also been a Visiting Professor at the Queen's University of Belfast, University of Ulster, Coleraine, and the Academy of Irish Cultural Heritages (Derry). He has written widely on Irish theatre, including articles on Dion Boucicault, Augusta Gregory, Brian Friel and Frank McGuinness. His *Brian Friel, Ireland and the North* (2007) is published by Cambridge University Press, and he is currently researching and writing on Belfast's Ulster Group Theatre.

**Dion Boucicault**

# Arrah-na-Pogue
# or, The Wicklow Wedding

**Methuen Drama**

Published by Methuen Drama 2010

1 3 5 7 9 10 8 6 4 2

Methuen Drama
A & C Black Publishers Limited
36 Soho Square
London W1D 3QY
www.methuendrama.com
Introduction copyright © 2010 Methuen Drama

ISBN 9781408146590

Available in the USA from Bloomsbury Academic &
Professional, 175 Fifth Avenue/3rd Floor, New York, NY 10010.
www.BloomsburyAcademicUSA.com

A CIP catalogue record for this book
is available from the British Library

Typeset by DC Graphic Design Ltd, Swanley Village, Kent

# Arrah-na-Pogue

## or, the Wicklow Wedding

# Introduction

To such fans of Dion Boucicault's Irish plays as Sean O'Casey, he is the father of a truly Irish theatre tradition; to others such as William Butler Yeats, he is responsible for the sentimental stage Irishman that the founders of the Abbey Theatre rejected. In either case, a more unlikely playwright of the Irish people could hardly be found. Although born in Dublin in 1820, he settled in London with his mother when he was barely eight years old, and until his death in 1890 he regularly lived in London or New York, but never again in Ireland. Nevertheless, according to his biographer Richard Fawkes, whenever he returned to Ireland, as he did briefly for performances in 1861 and 1864, 'he was welcomed back by his countrymen as a prodigal son', with 'crowds of admirers'.

When Boucicault started his career in the 1840s, he did not seek to become known as an Irish playwright; rather, he sought to establish himself in the English tradition of drawing-room comedies with such plays as *London Assurance* (1841) and *Old Heads and Young Hearts* (1844). While the young Boucicault did write several comedies with Irish themes or characters, such early works as *The Irish Heiress* (1842) or *Danny Blake, The Irish Diamond* (1854) failed on both the English and Irish stages. Rather, his early career is dominated by such sensational journalistic pieces as *The Poor of New York* (1857), which featured a tenement house ablaze and a real fire engine on stage, and *Jessie Brown; or, the Relief of Lucknow* (1858), which dramatised the Sepoy rebellion of 1857. By 1860, he had written nearly 80 plays, from the superficial *Agnes Robertson at Home* (1855) and which featured the singing and dancing talents of his young wife, and the borrowed in *Faust and Margaret* (1854), to even the lurid in *The Vampyre* (1852).

By all accounts, whether by attempting to renovate and manage a theatre in New Orleans or by merely living the life of a successful man about town in London, by 1860 Boucicault had made and squandered a fortune several times over.

Nevertheless, his experiences had not prepared him for the radical redirection of his career created by the extraordinary success of *The Colleen Bawn*, which was premiered at the Laura Keene Theater in New York City on 29 March 1860. During the late 1850s, Boucicault had written and appeared in several very popular plays, but *The Colleen Bawn* proved so successful in New York and Philadelphia that he decided to return to England with it after seven years in America. In an era when a play was considered a success if it held the stage for more than a week, *The Colleen Bawn* redefined the meaning of a 'long run' success. Not only was it performed every night at London's Adelphi Theatre for ten months and 230 performances, but Queen Victoria herself attended no less than three times. Recognising the magnitude of the play's success, Boucicault formed two touring companies to perform the play throughout Great Britain, he brought the play to Dublin in 1861, and by 1862 he recast the play as a successful opera, *The Lily of Killarney*.

Even when compared to the successes of the famous Irish actor Tyrone Power in the earlier decades of the century, *The Colleen Bawn* was the most popular Irish play of the century, and for Boucicault himself it inaugurated a more personal and nationalistic reorientation for his work. 'I have written an Irish drama for the first time in my life,' he was later to recall, a play that awakened him to 'Irish history and romance'. During the next thirty years he was to write a dozen more Irish plays, from the perennially popular *Arrah-na-Pogue* (1864) and *The Shaughraun* (1874), to the seditious *Amadan* (1883) and *Robert Emmet* (1884), with even a few flops among them in *Daddy O'Dowd* (1873) and *Fin Mac Coul* (1887). The success of these Irish plays transformed Boucicault himself as well, by awakening him to the theatrical potential of the Irishness that he had avoided throughout the first half of his career. According to his biographer Richard Fawkes, the young Boucicault largely abandoned acting in the early 1840s because his heavy Irish accent rendered him ill suited for many roles on the London stage. While he devoted his energies in the 1850s to writing works for his wife, the popular Agnes Robertson, and occasionally managing theatres, Boucicault limited himself as an actor to such exotic roles as the native chief Wahnotee in *The Octoroon* (1859) or the Moslem warrior Nana Sahib in *Jessie Brown* (1858).

In the rush to get *The Colleen Bawn* on the stage to replace his unsuccessful *Vanity Fair*, Boucicault assumed the role of Myles-na-Coppaleen, the play's lovelorn Irish peasant, and part of the play's astounding success resulted from Boucicault's talents embodying this charming Irish bootlegger. By taking this role, he embraced his long-neglected Irish identity, and by the mid-1870s he was identified with several charismatic Irish rogues, from Myles-na-Coppaleen to Shaun the Post in *Arrah-na-Pogue* (1864) and Conn in *The Shaughraun* (1874). As he aged, these roles became his most reliably popular, and in his final years when his other plays became unfashionable, they guaranteed him audiences and income.

However, his stage rebirth as iconic Irishman also awakened him to the politics of Irish nationalism. While these plays about Irish rogues, rebels and heiresses were surprisingly popular on the English stage, Boucicault came to publicly espouse nationalist opinions that were both unpopular, if not notorious, throughout England. For example, in 1874 he attempted to use the success of *The Shaughraun* to agitate for the release of Fenian prisoners, and in 1881 he published a pamphlet entitled *Ireland's Story*, which decried the history of English misrule in Ireland. In other words, for Victorian society Boucicault became the Irish rogue that he played on stage: loved by the Irish for plays that serve the English their comeuppance; loved by the English despite the blatant sedition that caused some of his plays to be banned by the Lord Chamberlain.

*Arrah-na-Pogue; or, The Wicklow Wedding* was premiered in Dublin in March 1864, mid-way through what the Irish historian

R.F. Foster described as a decade of 'Fenian fever' and less than three years before the failed rebellion of 1867. However, rather than retreating from the era's Irish grievances and long-smouldering issues associated with the English rule of the Irish, Boucicault addresses them directly. Moreover, his Victorian reviewers recognised that the views expressed in this play were Boucicault's own. Whereas most of his major plays throughout his career were liberal adaptions of Continental drama, Victorian novels or even contemporary events, *Arrah-na-Pogue* was 'that rarity, an original Boucicault play'.

*Arrah-na-Pogue* is set in the year of Ireland's most heroic uprising, the United Irishmen Rebellion of 1798. But, rather than locating the play in one of the many passive areas untouched by the scattered revolts, Boucicault sets the play in County Wicklow, an area briefly engulfed by the savage revolt in neighbouring Wexford, 'a campaign', according to R.F. Foster, 'marked by horrific and unforgotten atrocities on both sides'. Thus, while contemporary audiences may focus their attention on Boucicault's stage Irishman, Shaun the Post, the Victorian audience was concerned more with the competition between two forms of Irish heroism and two paradigms for Anglo-Irish relations. The play depicts the rivalry between two traditional Irish leaders, or sept heads: Beamish Mac Coul, a rebel who has returned from France to lead his men into revolt, and Bagenal O'Grady, who has become a colonel in the English army. Although they have taken opposing sides in this colonial dispute, Boucicault depicts them as united in their determined to protect the Irish poor from the English government's overwhelming and often misdirected power. Although these two noblemen do not share the stage until the play's final act, their fates steadily converge: not only do they both work to save Shaun the Post from undeserved punishment by the English government, but they both love the same woman, Fanny Power. And the play's climax allows them to join forces to educate the Colonial Secretary in the ways of the Irish, save Shaun from death and reconcile the rebel Mac Coul to the English government, all the while awaiting the news of which 'Irish gentleman' has won the love of Miss Power.

*Arrah-na-Pogue* came close to eclipsing the popularity of *The Colleen Bawn*: it held the stage for 168 performances in London and was toured throughout England and to Dublin, where it was performed for over three months. Within two years Boucicault travelled to Paris to oversee a French version of the play, and he frequently revived it throughout the 1860s and 1870s; indeed, its popularity seemed inexhaustible. In fact, just as he returned to England in 1860 to exploit the success of *The Colleen Bawn*, he returned to America in 1873 to stage both *Arrah-na-Pogue* and *The Colleen Bawn* together in dozens of cities on both American coasts and everywhere in between. Soon, these two plays, along with *The Shaughraun*, would form the Irish trilogy which became Boucicault's enduring accomplishment; even the Abbey Theatre's Frank Fay remarked in the early twentieth century that 'Dublin audiences never seem to weary' of Boucicault's Irish plays.

*The Shaughraun*, which premiered at Wallack's Theater in New York City on 14 November 1874, begins with the rumoured return of Robert Ffolliott, a Fenian leader of the revolt of 1867, from exile in Australia. But unlike Mac Coul in *Arrah-na-Pogue*, he seems to have no clear agenda for his return. Whereas Mac Coul used his time to train his men, bedevil the authorities and make plans to elope with Fanny Power, Ffolliott seems to have neither men to organise nor plans to implement. In fact, it soon becomes clear that Ffolliott is merely a naïve landowner who had been duped and betrayed by a local squireen who had designs on the young man's estate and fiancée. Of course, Ffolliott is saved by his loyal friend Conn the Shaughraun, and though the play largely keeps Ffolliott offstage and in prison, it allows Boucicault's character Conn ample opportunity to charm the audience both with his heroism and his histrionic antics.

We should not assume that Boucicault had lost interest in Irish nationalism or ardently Irish heroes. Rather, he uses this tale of innocence betrayed and delivered to win sympathy for a much more palatable form of Fenianism. Between the writing of *Arrah-na-Pogue* and *The Shaughraun*, the tensions between the English and the Irish had repeatedly erupted into violence. Not only had the Fenians attempted a revolt upon Irish soil in 1867, but they also launched attacks in England itself, including the assault on a police van transporting Fenians in Manchester and the bombing of Clerkenwell prison. There were even anti-Irish 'Murphy' riots in Birmingham, Lancashire and Ashton-under-Lyne; indeed, the unrest was so great that Karl Marx asserted that the English proletarian revolution would be sparked by the Irish tinderbox: 'I have come to the conclusion that the decisive blow against the ruling class in England [...] cannot be struck in England, but only in Ireland.'

But the revolution that would lead to Irish independence would not occur until twenty-five years after Boucicault's death, and it would not produce the type of Irish state that he envisioned in his plays. Nonetheless, despite his creation of the stage Irishman and valorisation of the Anglo-Irish, Boucicault remains something of the darling of Irish theatre. Indeed, film versions of his Irish trilogy became among the first movies filmed in Ireland when they appeared in 1911. Even the Abbey Theatre, which first was determined to distance itself from him, has staged *The Colleen Bawn*, *Arrah-na-Pogue* and *The Shaughraun* more than ten times since its first production of a Boucicault play, *The Shaughraun*, in 1967. It has even staged the opera based on *The Colleen Bawn*, *The Lily of Killarney*, as well as an Irish-language version of the play, *An Cailin Ban*.

**Scott Boltwood, November 2010**

# Arrah-na-Pogue

## or, the Wicklow Wedding

## Characters

**Shaun the Post**, *Driver of the Mail Car between Hollywood and Rathdrum*
**Colonel Bagenal O'Grady**, *The O'Grady*
**Beamish Mac Coul**, *The Mac Coul*
**Major Coffin**, *An English Officer*
**Michael Feeny**, *A Process Server*
**Secretary**
**Winterbottom**
**Sergeant**
**Oiny Farrell**
**Lanigan**
**Patsey**
**Andy Regan**
**Lanty**
**Moran**
**Tim Cogan**
**Arrah Meelish**, *nicknamed by the Peasantry Arrah-na-Pogue, or Arrah of the Kiss*
**Fanny Power**, *of Cabinteely*
**Katty Walsh**
**Soldiers** *and* **Peasants**


The Scene is laid in the County Wicklow in the year 1798.

# Act I

## Scene One

*Glendalough, Moonlight. The Ruins of St. Kevin's Abbey, the Round Tower, the Ruined Cemetery, the Lake and Mountains beyond; Music.*

**Beamish Mac Coul** *discovered.*

*Enter* **Oiny**.

**Oiny**   All right, sir; the car from Hollywood is in sight.

**Beamish**   How many passengers?

**Oiny**   There's only one, sir.

**Beamish**   That is our man. Hark ye, boys!

*Enter* **Lanty**, **Lanigan**, **Regan**, *and* **Morgan**.

**Beamish**   Take your stations so that you may give me timely warning of any alarm in the barracks yonder, or the approach of the patrol.

**Regan**   More power, sir.

**Oiny**   We'll be as 'cute as crows, yer honour.

**All**   Never fear, sir.

**Beamish**   Away with you!

*They retire.* **Lanty**, **Regan**, **Morgan**, **Lanigan**, **Oiny** *and two others.* **Beamish** *stands behind a part of the ruin.*

*Enter* **Feeny**.

**Feeny**   When a man thravels wid a big lump of money in his pocket, he is offering a reward for his own murdher. Why am I afeard? Sure this district is proclaimed; so divil a one dare set fut outside his cabin – dur afther nightfall widout a pass. And there below is the barrack, full of soldiers, widin the cast of my voice. (**Beamish** *appears.*) I'd like to see the skulkin' rebel that would show his nose on Derrybawn. (*Going as he speaks, finds*

**Beamish** (*opposed to him.*)   Oh, Lord!

**Beamish**   It is a fine night, Mr. Michael Feeny.

**Feeny**   So-o it is, long li-life to it; good night, sir. (*Trying to pass.*)

**Beamish**   Stop. You have just come from Hollywood, where you have collected the rents of an estate.

**Feeny**   Is it me? I'd be on me oath –

**Beamish**   Silence. The estates of the rebel Beamish Mac Coul were confiscated – your employer collects the rent for the Government, now I collect for the Mac Coul; so, hand over the amount.

**Feeny**   Is this robbery? and widin call of the barracks!

**Beamish**   If you lift your voice over a whisper to alarm the patrol, it will be murder as well as robbery. Not a word!

**Feeny** (*whispering*)   I wouldn't wake a weazel.

**Beamish**   Quick, the money!

**Feeny**   Whisht, you'll rise the soldiers, an' I'll be kilt. (*Drops on his knees.*) There's the money.

**Beamish**   Right. A bag of gold and a roll of notes. (*Receives the money from* **Feeny**.)

**Feeny** (*while* **Beamish** *examines it, aside*)   Oh, wait a bit, me time fellow, you can't move very far widout a pass; and only let me get safe out of this, and widin half an hour I will set a pack of redcoats on yer scent that will scour these hills and hunt the life out of ye.

**Beamish**   Good! Now your pass. (*Approaching* **Feeny**.)

**Feeny**   Me what?

**Beamish**   Your pass out with it – I want it to secure my free passage across the mountains.

**Feeny** (*giving* **Beamish** *papers*)   But how am I to get home widout it?

**Beamish**    There's your road. (*Pointing and putting him across.*)
At every fifty paces there's a man stationed behind either a rock
or a bush – he will see you straight to your door; and take a
friendly advice, don't turn from the path, nor speak a word till
you are safe in bed. Now be off!

**Feeny**    Oh, tare an' ages! Captain, dear, don't ax me to go
alone. Oh, murdher! Is it pass them file of divils? Are they
armed, Colonel?

**Beamish**    Each man has two blunderbusses on full cock, and
a bayonet pointed straight at you.

**Feeny**    I'm a corpse! Oh, Captain, Colonel, darlin', don't
lave me! Two blunderbushes lookin' at me, and a bagginet on
full cock. How will I get home at all ? I've got a canal running
down the middle of my back. I'm as wake as a wet rag this
minit.

**Beamish**    Come, off with you!

**Feeny**    I'm goin', sir. Where's my legs at all? Captain, jewel,
may I run?

**Beamish**    No, that would alarm the patrols, and seal your
fate.

**Feeny**    Oh, murdher, don't sale my fate, sir, and I'll creep
on my hands and knees; pass the word, Colonel, to kape
them quiet. Oh do, sir, give them the office. Oh, blessed day,
my inside is all fiddle-strings, and my blood is turnin' into
buttermilk.

*Exit.*

**Beamish**    Hush!

*Re-enter the men as before. They all run, looking after* **Feeny**; *then group.
When* **Beamish** *throws bag of money, it is caught by* **Oiny**.

**Beamish**    There he goes; we need fear no alarm from him.
I have turned every stone and every bush on his road into a
sentinel, ha, ha! Now, boys, divide this gold among ye. (*Throws*

*them the gold.*) You need not hesitate to take it, for the money is my own – I leave Ireland tomorrow, and forever. I could not part from you without giving you some token of my gratitude for the fidelity and love you have shown towards me.

**Oiny**   Ah, sir, wouldn't we pour out our blood, dhrop by dhrop, any day for the Mac Coul?

**Beamish**   I know it. For six weeks past I have found shelter on these hills under the noses of the military, while a reward of £500 offered for the capture of the rebel Beamish Mac Coul has not tempted your starvation to betray me.

**All**   Long life t'ye, sir; bless you always!

**Beamish**   See, the morning is beginning to tip the heights of Mullacor; we must part. In a few hours I shall be on the sea, bound for a foreign land; perhaps never again shall I hear your voices nor see my native hills. Oh, my own land! my own land! Bless every blade of grass upon your green cheeks! The clouds that over ye are the sighs of your exiled children, and your face is always wet with their tears. Eirne meelish, Shlawn loth fare ye well! And you, dear Abbey of St. Kevin, around which the bones of my forefathers are laid.

**Oiny**   Long life to them!

**All**   The Mac Coul! the Mac Coul!

*They crowd round him.*

**Beamish**   Easy boys, for your own sakes. No noise, no cries – let us part in silence. God bless you all!

**Regan**   Heaven keep you!

**All**   Blessins on you! May heaven be your bed! The good angels follow and surround ye always.

*He shakes hands with them.*

**Regan**   Hoult! the red-coats are on us.

**All**   Where?

*They crowd up.*

**Regan**   There! It's the dragoons, for I hear the horse peltin' up the boryeen.

**Beamish**   Do not be alarmed; the person who approaches is one who loves me so well that she leaves home, fortune, and friends to accompany the poor exile across the seas. So, whenever you remember Beamish Mac Coul in your prayers, don't forget to invoke a blessing also on the name of Fanny Power, of Cabinteely.

*Exit* **Beamish.**

**All**   Long life to ye both, sir!

**Oiny**   Now, boys, let us kape watch over the young masther while he is to the fore, and until we see him safe off.

**Regan**   I will hould the hill here below, and watch the barracks.

**Moran**   Lanigan and meself will watch the road to Laragh.

**Oiny**   The rest of us will be off to the cabin of Arrah-na-Pogue, where he finds shelther every night – and blessins on the brave girl that does not fear to face the gallows for his sake. Oh, it's small mercy they would show Arrah Meelish if it was known that she gave aid and protection to the outlaw, although he is her own foster-brother.

**Regan**   Bedad, if he was her own father and mother too, she'd hang for givin' them a God bless ye, if they wor what Beamish Mac Coul is this day.

**Oiny**   Here comes the masther – hurry now.

*Exeunt.*

*Re-enter* **Beamish** *with* **Fanny.**

**Beamish**   Dearest Fanny! is all prepared for our flight?

**Fanny**   Oh, Beamish, what will the world say of me? What will they think of me after I am gone?

**Beamish**  They will say that Beamish Mac Coul returned from his exile in France to claim the hand of the woman he loved; for the fairest woman in Wicklow had remained faithful to him during his four long years of absence.

**Fanny**  Can he say as much? Was he faithful to her during those four long years ?

**Beamish**  Do you doubt me?

**Fanny**  I wish I did not! For now you are going to take me goodness knows where. And if you grew weary of me, or fell in love with some foreign beauty with big eyes and a voice like silk velvet, what would become of me? Oh, Beamish, last night I took up a book to read, and there I found between the leaves an old love letter of yours I had placed as a marker there long ago, and I thought – Ah, maybe one day Beamish will leave me as I have left that letter as a mark in the middle of a love story, and shut me up with the tale only half read.

**Beamish**  Oh, very well, I see how it is. You have not sufficient confidence in me to entrust your fate in my keeping.

**Fanny**  No, it is not that.

**Beamish**  You wish me to remain here until you have made up your mind. You are not sure that you love me to the extent of the sacrifice of fortune, friends –

**Fanny**  Oh!

**Beamish**  Admirers! Yes, of course it is a great denial to relinquish the admiration – the worship of half the county.

**Fanny**  Oh, hear this.

**Beamish**  Very well. I will remain here until you love me better. I shall spend my days in the hollows of these rocks, or concealed in some tree; I pass my nights in some cave – cold, miserable, and alone.

**Fanny**   Oh! Beamish. I will go anywhere, do anything – my poor love. What a dreadful life you endure. Do you indeed sleep in a cave or up a tree? I wonder you are not frozen to death.

**Beamish**   I think of you, dearest; and that image is warmth, joy, and company.

**Fanny**   Don't! don't. I deserve all your reproaches for doubting you. And my hesitation prolongs such a miserable existence! Tell me what I am to do.

**Beamish**   Tonight, at an hour before midnight, meet me at the chapel near Tullabogue. There the ceremony of marriage will be performed, and before daylight we shall be on board a French craft, now lying off Bray Head, waiting my signal to assist in our escape.

**Fanny**   Well, I suppose I am in for it; but it feels very dreadful.

**Beamish**   Did you expect the banns would be published at St. Patrick's Cathedral, between Beamish Mac Coul, rebel, and Fanny Power, spinster?

**Fanny**   How cruel you are to laugh at my fears.

**Beamish**   When I ought to kiss them away.

**Fanny**   Hush! What noise was that?

*Enter* **Regan**.

**Regan**   Sir, sir, the pathrol is coming.

**Fanny**   The patrol! Fly, fly, Beamish!

**Beamish**   It is too late! – we must face the danger. They have seen us – see, they quicken their step.

**Regan**   More power, sir.

**Fanny**   Are you mad?

*Enter the* **Sergeant** *and file of Soldiers. One soldier bears a lantern.*

**Sergeant**   Halt! (*Advancing.*) Ho, my friend, what business have you abroad at this hour?

**Beamish**   Oh, Sergeant, have I not a beautiful excuse by me side? Look.

**Sergeant**   I don't want to see your excuse; I want to see your pass.

**Beamish**   Charmed to oblige you; there it is.

**Fanny** (*aside*)   I am dying of fright.

**Beamish** (*aside*)   Hold your tongue. He has got it upside down.

**Sergeant**   Quite correct, sir; sorry to be obliged to make these inquiries.

**Beamish**   I admire the precaution. Will you allow your men to drink this crown-piece to my health?

**Sergeant**   Sir, we are greatly obliged to you.

**Beamish**   I see you are going towards Laragh. Would you mind seeing me safe on my road? I am afraid these mountains are not at all secure for persons like me travelling with a large sum of money.

**Sergeant**   You will be quite safe with us. This way.

**Beamish**   And, Sergeant (*brings* **Sergeant** *forward a little*) if ever you meet me again, not a word of this little affair. You understand?

**Sergeant**   All right, sir! Mum's the word! Forward. March.

*Scene closes in.*


**Scene Two**

**Arrah**'s *Cottage at Laragh.*

**Shaun** *is heard singing outside.*

*Enter* **Shaun**.

**Shaun**   This is my weddin' mornin'; sure my breast is so big wid my heart this minit, that I feel like a fowl wid her first

egg. Egorra, and this same love brings a man out in a fine
perspiration, long life to it, And there's Arrah's cabin; the
oysther-shell that's got the pearl of my heart in it. I wonder is she
awake. (*Knocks.*) No signs of the chimney anyway. Arrah, suilis!
Arrah, mo millia stooreen! If you are slapin' don't answer me;
but if you are up, open the dure softly. (*He sings through the keyhole.*)
Open the dure softly,
Somebody wants ye, dear;
Give me a chink no wider than
You'll fill up wid your ear.
Or, if you're hard of hearing, dear,
Your mouth will do as well;
Just put your lips agan the crack,
And hear what I've to tell.
Open the dure, softly,
Somebody wants you, dear.

**Arrah** *opens the window.*

**Arrah**    Hur-roosh! hoo! that porkawn has got loose again, the
marauder!

**Shaun**    Is it the pig she takes me for?

**Arrah** (*aside*)    It's that thief o' the world, Shaun. (*Aloud.*) Or is it
the ould cow that's broke her sugaun? (*Calls.*) Coop, coop, coop!

**Shaun**    Another baste! Have I been singin' to the ould mare
till I've got a quadruped voice?

**Arrah** (*aside*)    Where is he hidin'? I'll take a peep. (*She puts out
her head; he catches her round the neck.*) Oh, murther! who's that?

**Shaun**    It's the pig that's got loose.

**Arrah**    Let me go, Shaun! D'ye hear me, sir? let me go!

**Shaun**    First I'll give ye the coward's blow. Come here, ye
vagabone, till I hit ye undher the nose wid my mouth.

**Arrah**    I'll sthrike back, ye villin! (*He kisses her; she pushes him
away.*) Isn't this purty thratement for a lone woman?

**Shaun**   Ye'll get no betther, now I warn ye; so don't go marryin' me this blessed day wid sthravagin expectations; ye'll have to live from hand to mouth, and whin you're out of timper I'll set my face agin you; mind that.

**Arrah**   You're back mighty early, Shaun; didn't you say that you had to dhrive Michael Feeny over from Hollywood last night?

**Shaun**   Sure enough; but he got down at Glendalough to walk across the hill.

**Arrah**   What brings ye up here at all, at all? Did ye think anybody was wantin' ye?

**Shaun**   Iss, indeed, ses I, 'There's that Colleen Dhas all alone, wid the cow to milk, and the pigs to feed, an chickeens; and the big barn beyant to get clane and swate by the evenin', for the weddin' tonight, an' not a ha'porth of help she'll take from mortial. I'll go and give her a lift'.

**Arrah**   Is it afther bein' up all night on the road betune Hollywood and Rathdrum; sure you have had no rest at all?

**Shaun**   Rest, darlin'! what would I want wid rest for the next six months to come? Wid the love in my heart that makes every minit a fortune, sure rest is only a waste of time, and to shut my eyes on the sight of your face before me is sinful exthravagance, my darlin'.

**Arrah**   Won't you rest sometimes, anyway?

**Shaun**   I'll look at you slapin', jewel, and that will do as well.

**Arrah**   Go on, now, ye comedtherin' schamer. Is it robbin' the beehives, or ating the honey clover, you have been, for you've the smell of it on your tongue? Go on, I tell ye. Dhrive the cow up from the field below, and maybe when you are back I'll lave a hot whate-male cake on the griddle to stop your mouth wid.

**Shaun**   Ah! there's a griddle in the middle of your own face,

Arrah, that has a cake on it always warm and ready to stop a boy's mouth.

**Arrah**   D'ye want me to bate ye, ye provoker? (*Beats him off.*) Oh, Shaun, cuishla agus machree, my heart goes wid ye and keeps stip beside you for ever and ever, my darlin'.

*Song –* **Arrah**: *'Oh, I love him dearly'.*

*Enter* **Beamish**.

**Beamish**   Has he gone?

**Arrah**   Oh, Masther Beamish, it goes sore agin me to be decavin' the poor boy this way. Isn't it better to let him know that it's yourself that's in it?

**Beamish**   My dear Arrah, if I were discovered in your cabin you know the penalty you would pay for the shelter and protection you have afforded the rebel.

**Arrah**   Ah, sir; but sure Shaun would lay down his life for you.

**Beamish**   Is it not enough that you should live with the halter round your neck, without including Shaun's foolish head in the same rope?

**Arrah**   And would they hang him for only knowing that you were here to the fore?

**Beamish**   Ay, would they – both you and he together – and although this day is your wedding-day, that's not the sort of noose you expect to get into.

**Arrah**   Bedad it's not!

**Beamish**   Then don't deceive yourself. While I remain here you and I are standing under the same gibbet.

**Arrah**   I'm proud to stand anywhere beside yourself Master Beamish; and sure isn't the cabin there your own, anyway? 'Twas your gift to my mother that nursed you. You were fostered under that old thatch itself; and if they tuk and hung me to the dure-post beyant, sure my life 'ud be the only rint we ever paid the Mac Coul for all the blessins we owe the ould family.

**Beamish** Hold out your hands. (*Places money in them.*) There.

**Arrah** What's this?

**Beamish** It is my wedding-gift; the marriage portion you will bestow on Shaun this day.

**Arrah** Bank-notes! But, oh, sir, why would I take this from yourself, and you so poor?

**Beamish** That is precisely the reason you cannot refuse it. Sure, if I was rich, there would be less pleasure to me in giving it you, goose.

**Arrah** But how will tell Shaun that I came by so much money?

**Beamish** In three days I shall be in France; till then answer no questions. Then you may tell him all.

**Arrah** Well, I promise; but he'll never forgive me. It'll be a sore place wid him agin me.

**Beamish** I'll engage you'll find a way of drawing out the pain.

**Arrah** Faith, I've a notion I will.

**Beamish** Now I must return till dark to my nook in the barn, where I roost under the thatch, where my only companion is the cat.

**Arrah** Ah! sir, why have I not as many lives as they say she has? I'd give the whole nine of them for your sake.

**Beamish** I know it.

*Exit into cottage.*

**Arrah** He's goin' away to the wild wars, wid death and danger by the wayside. Shall I ever see him agin after this night? Oh! My brother! May the sweet angels of heaven put out the fire of the guns, and turn away the bagginets foreninst ye!

*Enter* **Feeny**.

**Feeny**   Where is Shaun?

**Arrah**   How would I know? (*Close windows.*)

**Feeny**   Aisy, now, Arrah. As I come over the top of the hill beyant, sure I saw ye both on this spot, colloguin togithir.

**Arrah**   Did ye? I hope the sight was plazin' to ye sir.

**Feeny**   And as I turned the corner there, I saw the tail of his coat as he went into the cabin.

**Arrah** (*aside*)   'Twas Master Beamish.

**Feeny**   Ah! Arrah, it's the bad luck that is over me entirely this day. There's yourself that I love, wid all my heart!

**Arrah**   That's not sayin' much.

**Feeny**   And this blessed day I'm goin' to be robbed of you!

**Arrah**   Whisht! he'll hear ye.

**Feeny**   Shaun, is it? D'ye think I'm ashamed of my love for you?

**Arrah**   No; but I am. I wouldn't like him to think so manely of me as to feel that you love me. (*Goes up to pail.*)

**Feeny**   Well, I'm a poor thing entirely. Bedad! one would think I was a disorder that was catchin'; but maybe you'll repint the hour you made little of me, for I can wait, my darlin'; and to them that waits their time comes round, and when mine comes I'll make you feel a little of what I feel now.

**Arrah**   If Shaun heard them words he'd have to answer for your life.

**Feeny**   Let him answer first for my money! This mornin' on Derrybawn, not five minutes after I left his car, I was waylaid and robbed by twenty blackguards that lay ready for me.

Who but Shaun knew that I had the rents of Hollywood in my pocket? Who but he knew the hour and the place where I could be caught?

**Arrah**    Robbed! and by Shaun! What could he want wid your dirty money?

**Feeny**    He'd want it for you, marm, if you please.

**Arrah**    Be all that's mane, I believe the crature thinks that sweet-hearts pay one another, and ye can buy a ha'porth of love at the hucksther's shop. Look here, man! d'ye see that? (*Shows him the money she received from* **Beamish**.) It isn't money we want.

**Feeny**    Oh! what's that?

**Arrah**    Look! l0 and 5, and 10 agin, and 3 and 5 once more. Look! that's right; I know the sight warms your heart.

**Feeny**    Can I believe my eyes?

**Arrah**    I thought I'd astonish you.

**Feeny** (*aside*)    They are the same that a few hours ago I was robbed of on Derrybawn. (*Aloud.*) Let me look agin.

**Arrah**    Oh, look and feel! Don't you long that they were yours?

**Feeny** (*examining a note*)    Yes; here's my own name upon the back. (*Returns it to her.*)

**Arrah**    Now, you see we don't want your money, nor your company aither. There's your road; (*points off*) it is waitin' for ye. Good mornin'!

*Exit into cottage.*

**Feeny**    Shaun is one of the gang that robbed me – divil a doubt of it. I'll swear to them notes; and there he is inside wid her this minute! Stop! I'll take a peep, that I may make oath I saw himself. (*Goes to cabin.*) Oh! tare alive! but this is too good to be thrue. I don't desarve it. (*Looks through keyhole into cabin.*)

**Shaun** (*entering*)   Well, bad luck to her for a cow! Ah! you're the only female of your sex I never could make any hand of at all.

**Feeny**   Divil a thing I see but the dark.

**Shaun**   What's that? (*Sees* **Feeny**.)

**Feeny**   Yes; there he is! Now I see him!

**Shaun**   Do ye? (*Seizing him behind by collar of coat and seat of his britches.*) Well, and d'ye feel him, you spyin' vagabone? (*Shaking him.*)

**Feeny**   What's this, Shaun? I thought – I mean – I – ain't you inside the cabin?

**Shaun**   No! I don't find it convanient to be in two places at onst.

**Feeny**   And it wasn't you that was here, and it is somebody else that – phew! (*Aside.*) What's all this at all? Oh, tare and ages, I smell a rat.

**Shaun**   Now, Michael Feeny, listen hether, and take a friendly warning. This day will make me masther of that cabin and all that's in it; and if I find your nose in my kayhole, be the tongs of the devil I'll lave ye nothin' to blow for the rest of your dirty life.

*Enter* **Arrah** *from cottage.*

**Arrah**   Shaun!

**Feeny** (*aside*)   She is bothered.

**Arrah**   What is the matter!

**Feeny**   It's only a mistake; I thought Shaun was inside there wid yerself – didn't ye tell me he was?

**Arrah**   No, I didn't.

**Feeny** (*aside*)   She's tremblin'. (*Aloud.*) I was thinkin' you said 'twas he gave you all the money you showed me.

**Shaun**   What money is he talkin' about?

**Arrah**  Ah, never mind him.

**Feeny** (*aside*)  She's frightened; there's a man hidin' widin' there, that Shaun knows nothing about. 'Twas he, not Shaun, that gav' her the money – 'twas he that robbed me. Oh, Arrah Meelish, I have ye now. Ye despise me, do you – well, I'll bring you down to my feet, low as I am. I'll show you to all the neighbours, wid your fine lover hidin' in your cabin, and we'll see which you like best round your purty neck – my arms or the felon's rope, my jewel.

**Shaun**  When you and the divil have done colloguin together, I'd like to see the full front of your back.

**Feeny**  The top of the mornin' t'ye both.

*Exit.*

**Shaun**  Well, sweet bad luck go wid ye, and that's my blessin' on ye.

**Arrah**  Ah, never mind him, dear! it's thrue what he said about the money, and here it is, Shaun. It is a present I got on my weddin' day.

**Shaun**  What's this? Oh, Biddy Mulligan! Bank-notes; and have you found a crock o' goold full of bank-notes, or did ye catch a leprichaun, an' squeeze this out of him between your finger and thumb?

**Arrah**  Yes, indeed, it was one of the good people that gav' it to me, and he tould me not to tell you a word about it for three days – them's the conditions I recaved wid it. (*Going.*)

**Shaun**  Well, that's an asy way ov risin' money: three days! Can ye get any more of it on the same conditions? Make it six, dear, and divil a word I'll ax, but open my mouth and shut my eyes, and let it roll down widout a wink. Powdhers of war! Arrah! what am I marryin' at all? Beauty and wealth, no less. It's my belief you are a fairy, born and bred. Your mother was sweet Vanus herself, and your father was the Bank of Ireland.

*Exit.*

## Scene Three

*The Armoury in* **O'Grady**'s *House.*

*Enter* **Fanny Power**.

**Fanny**   I have managed to regain my room without discovery
Well! this is nice behaviour for a young lady! The inmate of
a respectable house to be scampering over the country by
moonlight. I wonder I'm not ashamed of myself! And this is
my wedding-day! I must spend it in deceit and fear! not daring
to look in the face of those that love and trust me. After dark,
dressed in an old cloak, I must creep away like a thief to be
married by rushlight in an old ruin; then I'll be hurried on
board a dirty smuggler, among fifty strange men, who will
know all I've been at. This is a nice programme.

*Enter* **O'Grady** *with a letter.*

**O'Grady**   Congratulate me, my dear Fanny. This is the
happiest day of my life.

**Fanny**   Then you are not going to be married?

**O'Grady**   You must let me hope that I am. D'ye remember
about six months ago – I mean the last time you refused me?

**Fanny**   Haven't I refused you since then? Well.

**O'Grady**   You said to me: 'O'Grady! never pronounce the
word love to me again until you bring me the royal pardon of
Beamish Mac Coul.'

**Fanny**   And did not my anxiety awake any jealous feelings in
your breast?

**O'Grady**   Not in the least. Sure I knew that your interest
sprang from the romantic sympathy of your little seditious
heart for the rebel and not from any love for a man you never
saw; so I set to work, and mighty hard work it was!

**Fanny**   Do you mean to tell me that you have succeeded?
Oh, dear Bagenal, are there hopes?

**O'Grady**   Fanny! if you talk and look at me like that I'll ring for help.

**Fanny**   Speak, you dearest of injured mortals!

**O'Grady**   I have accomplished the task you imposed upon me, and you are free to reward me. Don't be overcome, Fanny; I am yours.

**Fanny**   I am bewildered with joy.

**O'Grady**   Here is the letter from the Secretary of State. (*Reads.*) 'My dear Colonel – In consideration of your eminent services –'

**Fanny**   Oh, never mind that – to the point!

**O'Grady**   This is the point. 'In considera – (*She snatches the letter.*)

**Fanny** (*reads*)   Um-um! Ah! 'The matter was brought before the Council'. So. 'A free pardon is granted to young Mac Coul, provided he is not implicated in the fresh disturbances which once more threaten to agitate your neighbourhood'.

**O'Grady**   Fortunately, Beamish is in France, so that proviso cannot apply to him. There's the pardon – the life of your hero. What's the next step?

**Fanny**   Throw it in the fire.

**O'Grady**   Upon my conscience, Fanny, I believe that you're a book of Euclid and not a woman at all, for there's no understanding you.

**Fanny**   Is there not? Well, tonight you will understand me, and then you will know upon what a deceitful, unworthy, baggage you have thrown away your generous heart.

**O'Grady**   By all the love that's in me, Fanny, what makes you the most perfect in my eyes is your faults, and the weak points of your character are the most irresistible. (*Noise outside.*) What is that agreeable uproar?

*Enter* **Patsey**.

**Patsey**   Plase your honour, it's the weddin' party from Laragh – Shaun the Post and Arrah Meelish, wid all their followin', are on their way to the chapel, sir.

**O'Grady**   Show them in, Patsey. (*Exit* **Patsey**.) I suppose the young couple want my license to keep open house tonight to regale their friends.

**Fanny**   Are they followers of the O'Grady?

**O'Grady**   No they belong to the sept of the Mac Coul.

**Fanny**   Ah!

*Re-enter* **Patsey**, *and enter* **Shaun**, **Arrah**, *and Village Girls and Men.*

**All**   Long life to you, sir.

**Arrah**   It is the smile of fortune we bring, your honour. May the grass never grow on your dure step, nor fail on your hills. May your hearthstone be always as warm as your heart; and when you die may the wail of the poor be the only sorrow of your life!

**O'Grady**   Now, Shaun, what's the good word from you?

**Shaun**   Well, your honour, seein' the sweet lady that's by your side, I can think of nothin' else to say but 'More power t'ye, and long life to enjoy it!'

**All**   Hurroo!

**O'Grady**   Thank ye, Shaun; and may this day that will change the name of your bride never change the heart of Arrah-na-Pogue!

**Fanny**   Arrah-na-Pogue! that means Arrah-of-the-Kiss!

**O'Grady**   Don't you know why she is called so? Tell her, Arrah.

**Arrah**   Sure I do be ashamed, sir.

**Shaun**　Ah! what for? It's proud I am of the kiss you gave, though it wasn't meself that got the profit of it.

**Fanny**　Indeed; and who was the favoured one?

**Shaun**　Beamish Mac Coul, Miss; her comdaltha – I mane her, foster-brother, that is. It was four years ago. He was lyin' in Wicklow Gaol day before he was to be hung wid the rest of us in regard of the rising.

**Fanny**　I remember, he escaped from prison the day before his execution.

**Shaun**　Thrue for ye, miss. The boys had planned the manes of it, but couldn't schame any way to give him the office, because no one was let in to see the masther, barrin' they wor sarched, and then they could only see his face at a peep-hole in the dure of his cell.

**Fanny**　Did Arrah succeed in conveying to him the necessary intelligence?

**Shaun**　She did. Bein' only a dawny little crature that time, they didn't suspect the cunnin' that was in her; so she gave him the paper in spite of them, and under the gaoler's nose.

**Fanny**　How so? You say they searched her. Did they not find it?

**Shaun**　No, miss; you see they didn't search in the right place. She had rowled it up and put it in her mouth; and when she saw her foster-brother, she gave it to him in a kiss.

**Arrah**　And that's why they call me Arrah-na-Pogue.

**Fanny**　No one but a woman would have thought of such a post-office.

**Shaun**　That's the only post-office I mean to get my letters from the rest of my life. (*Laugh.*)

**Arrah**　It's a poor thing I did for him that has done so much for Shaun and me. We owe him every feet of land that gives us bread, and the roof that covers us. There isn't a hap'orth we have but belongs to him.

**Fanny** (*aside*)  How her face blushes, and her eyes fill as she speaks of him.

**O'Grady**  Well, Shaun, I suppose you want a magistrate's permission to keep open house tonight? You shall have it. Patsey, put a keg or two of liquor on the car; if I can't attend in person at your feast, I will be there in spirit anyway.

**All**  Long life t'ye, sir. The O'Grady for ever. Hurroo!

*Exeunt.*

**O'Grady**  Here's another woman infatuated with the Mac Coul. It is wonderful.

**Fanny**  I'm uneasy about myself. I thought I was his only case – I hope he is not an epidemic.

*Re-enter* **Patsey**.

**Patsey**  Major Coffin, sir.

**O'Grady**  I am delighted to see him.

*Enter* **Major Coffin**.

**O'Grady**  No bad news from the disturbed districts I hope, Major?

**Major** (*bowing*)  Miss Power, I'm yours. Colonel, my news is excellent. The French emissary, whose presence in this neighbour-hood we have for six weeks suspected, but who has eluded our efforts to trace –

**O'Grady**  Because no such person is to be found.

**Fanny** (*aside*)  'Tis Beamish!

**O'Grady**  Well, Major, is there any news of your wild goose?

**Major**  The most precise. We have discovered his nest. A thousand pardons, Miss Power, for entering on such a matter in your presence.

**Fanny**  Not at all – I beg you to proceed. I – I am more

deeply interested in your success than you can imagine. You have not – caught the – the rebel?

**Major**   Had we done so, I beg to assure you, the first tree would have settled his business, without occupying your attention with such a vagabond. (*To the* **O'Grady**.) Do you know the collecting clerk of the Government Agent, one Mr. Michael Feeny?

**O'Grady**   I do! – well; he's the biggest thief in the county Wicklow, and that's the best I know of him.

**Major** (*calls*)   Step this way, Mr. Feeny.

*Enter* **Feeny**.

**O'Grady**   Oh! Mr. Feeny, I think we are acquainted; when last we met I introduced myself.

**Feeny**   Yes, Colonel; I think – I – that is – you –

**O'Grady**   I kicked you from the hall – door to the lodge-gate, for serving a process on a guest of mine.

**Feeny**   I am afraid, Colonel, that I left an unfavourable impression on you.

**O'Grady**   I am sure, sir, I left a number of unfavourable impressions on you. What does this fellow want?

**Major**   He alleges that last night he was robbed by fifty armed men on Derrybawn Hill. His description of their leader tallies with that of the man of whom we are in search. By accident he has traced part of the plunder, and discovered, at the same time, the rebel's nest.

**O'Grady**   Poor devil! Well, I suppose you want me to hear this fellow's depositions? If you will step into the justice-room, I am sure Miss Power will excuse us. This way, Major.

*Exeunt.*

**Fanny** (*alone*)    Is it Beamish they seek! He was on Derrybawn last night, and that wretch has tracked him, and marked him down, in some cave or up a tree, where he lies now, little expecting the fate that awaits him. Can I hear what they say? (*Listens at the door.*) Yes ! – hush! – he speaks! he recognized the notes to be the same of which he was robbed! Eh? What does he say? In the possession of Arrah Meelish ? – Arrah, the girl that was here just now! Hush! The rebel chief is her lover, and he is concealed in her cabin at Laragh! Oh! what have I heard? Beamish there! No! it is not possible. Yet how the girl's face beamed when she spoke of him, Ah! They return.

*Re-enter* **O'Grady**, **Major Coffin** *and* **Feeny**.

**Major**    I propose to make a descent on this girl's cabin tonight.

**O'Grady**    Tonight! and this is her wedding-day, poor thing! Couldn't you put it off till tomorrow?

**Major**    And risk the escape of our man?

**Feeny**    Oh! divil a fear o' that, your honour; the cabin is well watched this minute by them that won't let a mouse stir out of it widout givin' the alarm. We've got him safe enough.

**Fanny** (*aside*)    How, then, can I warn him of his danger?

**O'Grady**    Major, speaking from experience, I believe that fellow is lying. The truth would be ashamed to be seen coming out of him. I know the girl he has denounced, and I'll pledge my honour for hers.

**Fanny**    And I'll pledge mine for the man. No! I mean, I – I – I don't think it possible any woman could be so base.

**O'Grady**    What do you know about it?

**Fanny**    I am only saying what you say; and you are not going to turn round now, and say otherwise because I say so too?

**Major**    If she is innocent, investigation can only confirm your good opinion, in which I am resolved to share.

**O'Grady**  Then I will go with you!

**Fanny**  So will I.

**O'Grady**  You, Fanny!

**Fanny**  Yes! I cannot restrain the interest I feel in this investigation. I will not believe that a man can be so base to maintain a love affair up to his very wedding day; and with such a secret in his breast abuse the honest heart of one who loves him.

**O'Grady**  But it isn't a man; it is a woman.

**Fanny**  Well, it is all the same thing. Don't annoy with your fine distinctions. Come, Major, let me hear the particulars from yourself; for the O'Grady gets so confused when he attempts to explain anything, that my understanding becomes as muddled as his own.

*Exit with* **Major**.

**O'Grady**  Tender-hearted angel! See how she stands up for one of her own sex in trouble!

**Feeny**  I hope, Colonel, dear, you will disremember the little matter betune us, sir, and not hould it agin me; I'm only a tool, sir, in my employer's hands, and sixteen shillins a week is all I get for the dirty work.

**O'Grady**  Then you get more kicks than ha'pence. Stand outside the gate, my man, and don't let the dogs smell ye.

*Exit.*

**Feeny**  Aha! oho! Arrah-na-Pogue. I tould ye that I'd take down that purty nose of your own, that ye turned up at me when I axed ye to say the word. It's a grand weddin' ye'll have, my lady; but it is in Wicklow Gaol ye'll pass this night! I tould you my time would come, and that I would bring ye to my fut, and when ye rise from that it shall be into my arms.

*Exit.*

## Scene Four

*A Barn attached to **Arrah**'s Cabin at Laragh. Through the wide-open door the Village is seen, dotted with lights, and straggling up the Valley towards Glendalough, which is visible in the distance. The Ruins and Round Tower are also seen beyond the Village.*

**Beamish** (*descends staircase*)   This place is watched. Has my retreat been discovered? When the wedding party returns, I can mix unnoticed with the crowd, and escape in the dark. (*Music and shouts outside.*) Here they come. (*He ascends to the loft.*)

*Enter a procession, preceded by Beggars and Children, then a Piper and Fiddlers; then the Bridesmaids and Men; then **Shaun** and **Arrah** in a car, with the Priest; then a Crowd.*

**Shaun**   A kind welcome to every mother's son of ye, and a warmer one agin to every petticoat. Bad luck to the first that laves the house, barrin' he doesn't know any better.

**All**   Hurroo!

**Shaun** (*music during this*)   There's lashins of mate inside, and good liquor galore, and him that spares what's there I look upon as my inimy. (*He jumps on a barrel – music again. Exeunt all into inner room, **Arrah** first, with the Priest as they go in.*) Pat Ryan lave that girl alone till the grace is said; in wid ye, you are welkim as the flowers in May. Nora Kavinagh, don't be provokin' that boy before he's able for ye. Ah! Tim Conolly, is it cologuin wid two girls at a time you are: I'm lookin' at ye. Walk in, my darlins, and cead mille failtha. (*He leaps down and follows them.*)

*Re-enter **Arrah**; she looks round cautiously.*

**Arrah**   Are ye gone, sir?

**Beamish** (*appearing on the stairs, and leaning over*)   From my trap-door in the roof above, I can see men in the road below, who seem to be watching this place. Surely they cannot suspect my retreat here? Who could have betrayed me?

**Arrah**   From the roof of the barn you can rache a tree, and by its branches climb to the rock above.

**Beamish**   I won't try that except as a last experiment. Oh!
Arrah, if I were caught here, what would become of you?

**Arrah**   Never mind me, save yourself.

**Beamish**   Come what may I must be at Tullabogue in two
hours from this time (*cries and laughter within*) – but don't let me
detain you from the feast. Good-bye, we may not see each
other again, so heaven bless and preserve you. May heaven
keep you – farewell!

**Arrah**   Good-bye, sir. (*He disappears.*) He is going, and while
they are hunting the life out of him, here am I dancing and
marryin', and laffin', wid no more feeling in me than if I wor
a wet sod of turf that hasn't a ha'porth of warmth in its heart,
although ye stick it in the middle of the fire.

*Enter* **Shaun**, *door.*

**Shaun**   Where are ye at all? Oh! it is alone we are for a
blessed minute itself; and I have ye all to myself, my darlin',
my own that ye are, now. Oh, murther! when I luk at you, so
clean and nate, and purty, it's fit you are for a bit of chaney on
the chimbly-piece of the quality in a drawing-room, not for
my dirty cabin. And how did you come to love a poor ignorant
cratur like meself, at all, at all?

**Arrah**   Poor and ignorant! How dar' ye be calling my
husband names?

**Shaun**   Iss, poor I am; I never knew it till I saw you inside my
dure. Ignorant, I am; I never felt it till I thried to tell ye what
was in my heart, and found I hadn't larnin' to do it, anyway.
No! I can't make it out at all, unless you are a fairy that has
stooped to make fun of a poor boy. I'm expectin' every minute
to see your wings breakin' out behind upon ye; and maybe
you'll rise up like a butterfly, and be off to the skies above,
where you belong.

**Arrah**   Ah Shaun, my darlin', don't spake to me that way –
don't make so much of me.

**Shaun**   Oh, my threasure! Oh, mo storreen bheg! If there was a diamond as big as yourself, it would be a poor thing beside you, my darlin'. But what's the matter, dear? Is it cryin' you are? Oh, is it anything I've said, bad luck to me, that's made ye cry, my darlin'?

**Arrah**   No! no! don't ax me.

**Shaun**   I won't dear – av coorse – why would I? Ye see, I'm not used to the tindher and soft ways of women, an' if I'm rough or wrong any way, won't ye tell me till I larn how to behave (*all enter slowly*) – for sure if I didn't spake to you like that, sure my heart is so big in my breast it would choke me, my dear. I do be afraid to go near some girls for fear of spoilin' their new and beautiful clothes; but I'm afraid of touchin' you for fear of spoilin' the bloom on your fresh and beautiful sowl.

**Arrah**   Oh, Shaun! when I listen to you talkin' to me that way, you make me feel so small beside ye. (*He kisses her.*)

*Enter Crowd.*

**All**   Oh! we caught ye – ha! ha! ha! (**Arrah** *pushes* **Shaun** *away.*)

**Shaun**   Is a good example to be thrown away upon ye? Boys, when the bride gets her first kiss, sure, it's a kiss all round.

*A scramble among the girls and boys.*

**Oiny**   More power, yer souls! here's old Tim Cogan, of Ballimore, says he'll take the flure agin any famale ov his age and sex in the company.

**Shaun**   Whoo! d'ye hear that! For the honour of the County Wicklow, isn't there a pair of brogues undher a petticoat that will stand up agin the County Kildare?

**Katty**   Come out o' that, Tim Cogan, till I take the consate out of yiz.

**All**   Hurroo for Katty! Katty Walsh, aboo!

**Shaun**   Aisy, now, ye rapparees. Katty, darlin', let me lade ye out. It's yourself that'll stretch Tim Cogan like a dead fowl this blessed evenin', if you'll put it to him sthrong before he gets his second wind. What shall be the time of it, avourneen?

**Katty**   'Fatther Jack Welsh' agin the world.

**Shaun**   That's the daisy; and it's yirself will tatther Tim Cogan, I'll go bail. Would ye take a sup first, or will ye dance dhry? There's a one-pound note among the fiddlers if the lady is plazed wid the tune of it.

**All**   Hurroo!

**Shaun**   Now, ye scrapin' thieves, pull out the plug and run it sthrong. (*Dance. A jig by* **Katty** *and* **Tim Cogan**.) Whoo! that's iligant! Welt the flure, Katty.

**Oiny**   Hould up to her, Tim.

**Shaun**   Cover the buckle fair, ye ould schamer.

**Regan**   Kildare for a tinpenny.

**Shaun**   Ah, don't decave yerselves; Katty is only jokin'. Wait till she offers her fut to him. Whoo! that's the sthroke!

**Regan**   Hould up the credit of the county, Tim.

**Shaun**   Put your back into it, Katty; his off-leg is a Quaker. Stick to him, my jewel, he's goin'; he goin'.

**Tim** *falls exhausted. A shout from all the crowd.*

**Katty**   Whoo! (*Dances around him amidst general applause, and is led ceremoniously by* **Shaun** *to a seat – he hands her a jug of punch.*)

**Shaun**   Now, boys, one glass all round, and then I'll call upon Paddy Finch for a song.

**All**   Whoo! Where's Pat? Pat, ye schamer, clare yer pipes. Paddy, yer wantin'.

**Oiny**   If ye plaze, here he is; but not a note ye'll get out of him this night, barrin' it's a snore. He's overtaken.

**Shaun**   Is he salted down intirely?

**Kaily**  He is contint.

**Arrah**  Come, Shaun, for want of a betther, we'll take a song from yourself.

**All**  Hurroo! Rise it, Shaun, avich.

**Shaun**  Will, ladies, it's for you to choose the time of it. What shall it be?

**Regan**  'The Wearing of the Green.'

**All**  Hurroo!

**Shaun**  Whisht, boys, are ye mad? is it sing that song and the soldiers widin gunshot? Sure there's sudden death in every note of it.

**Oiny**  Niver fear; we'll put a watch outside and sing it quiet.

**Shaun**  It is the 'Twistin' of the Rope' ye are axin' for?

**Regan**  Divil an informer is to the fore – so out wid it.

**Shaun**  Is it alright outside there?

**Oiny** (*advancing*)  Not a sowl can hear ye, barrin' ourselves.

**Shaun**  Murdher alive! kape lookin' out.

*Song – 'The Wearing of the Green'.*

O Paddy dear, and did you hear the news that's going round?
The shamrock is forbid by law to grow on Irish ground;
St. Patrick's Day no more we'll keep, his colours can't be seen,
For there's a bloody law again the wearing of the green.
I met with Napper Tandy, and he took me by the hand,
And he said, 'How's poor old Ireland, and how does she stand?'
She's the most distressful country that ever yet was seen,
They are hanging men and women for the wearing of the green.

Then since the colour we must wear is England's cruel red,
Sure Ireland's sons will ne'er forget the blood that they have shed.
You may take the shamrock from your hat and cast it on the sod,
But 'twil take root and flourish there, though under foot 'tis trod.

When law can stop the blades of grass from growing as they grow,
And when the leaves in summer time their verdure dare not show,
Then I will change the colour that I wear in my caubeen,
But till that day, please God, I'll stick to wearing of the green.

But if at last our colour should be torn from Ireland's heart,
Her sons with shame and sorrow from the dear old isle will part;
I've heard a whisper of a country that lies beyond the sea
Where rich and poor stand equal in the light of freedom's day.
O Erin, must we leave you, driven by a tyrant's hand?
Must we ask a mother's blessing from a strange and distant land?
Where the cruel cross of England shall nevermore be seen,
And where, please God, we'll live and die still wearing of the
    green.

**Arrah**  Well, this is purty goings on at my weddin'. Boys, I am
spoilin' for a dance, and not one-among ye has axed me the
time I'd like, nor offered to provoke my fut to the flure. Oiny
Farrell, stand out and face me if ye dar. Come, girls, the
fiddlers are ashamed of ye.

**All**  Hurroo!

*They take their places for a jig, the fiddlers commence playing. A drum
heard outside; general consternation. Enter a file of Soldiers, led by
the* **Sergeant***; he disposes of the men so as to surround the cabin.*
**Beamish***, who has been visible during the previous scenes in the loft
formed by the rafters of the barn, now is seen to throw off his coat, and to
open the trap-door in the roof he disappears through it.*

*Enter* **Major Coffin**, **The O'Grady**, **Fanny Power**, *and* **Feeny**.

**Major**  Guard the doors; let no one pass.

**O'Grady**  We are sorry to disturb your diversions, boys, but
a robbery was committed last night on Derrybawn Hill, and we
have received information that some of the plunder has been
traced to this spot.

**Shaun**  Is it a thief you are afther, sir? Ah, thin, if any such a
one is undher this roof, ye are welcome to him.

**Major**    Now, Mr. Feeny, whom do you charge with having possession of the plunder?

**Feeny**    That woman, Arrah Meelish.

**All**    Arrah!

**Feeny** (*advancing*)    Oh, never fear; we'll find the money in her pocket. Let her be searched.

**Shaun** (*turning and seizing* **Feeny**)    Lay a finger on her and I'll brain ye!

**Major**    Arrest that fellow! (**Sergeant** *advances towards* **Shaun**.)

**O'Grady** (*interposing*)    'Asy, Major; what would you do if a man offered to lay a hand on the woman you loved? Be the powers, I'd have brained him first and warned him aftherwards. Shaun, my man, the thing is settled in a moment. We don't believe a word this fellow has deposed, but if Arrah has any money – bank-notes about her –

**Shaun**    She has, sir.

**O'Grady**    See that! Then let us just look at them.

**Shaun**    Wid all the pleasure in life. Arrah, dear, gi'me them notes you showed me a while ago. Don't be frightened, darlin'. Come.

**Arrah** *gives* **Shaun** *the notes with trembling reluctance.*

**O'Grady** (*receiving the notes from* **Shaun**)    The Bank of Naas.

**Feeny**    And they are part of them that I was robbed of last night on Derrybawn. I'll swear to them. Luk and you'll find my name on the back of one o' them. There, that's the one. See! d'ye believe me now?

**O'Grady**    Where and from whom did you receive this money?

*A pause.*

**Shaun** (*aside*)    Why doesn't she spake?

**O'Grady**   I'm sure you won't refuse to tell us how you became possessed of these notes. (*A pause.*) Afther what you have heard, if you are innocent, as I am sure you are, you won't help to screen the thief!

*The **Major** advances to **Arrah**.*

**Major**   You are silent. Well, then, perhaps you will answer another question. Where is the young man who has been concealed in your cabin for the last six weeks? (**Arrah** *clasps her hands over her face. A murmur amongst the crowd. Peasants whisper to each other.*) Do you hear me? I want the young man – your lover, the secret leader of the rebel movement in this neighbourhood – who committed this robbery last night, and then shared with you the proceeds of his crime.

**Shaun**   Arrah!

**Arrah**   Shaun, let me spake to ye.

**Major**   No; you are my prisoner. This girl must hold no communication with any here. (*Two soldiers advance and arrest her, while a third unlocks a pair of handcuffs.*) Search this place.

**Feeny**   I know every hole and corner in it. Folly me.

**Sergeant** *and two soldiers go out. Two, led by* **Feeny**, *ascend the staircase, and are seen in the loft above, thrusting their bayonets into the sacks and trusses of straw, etc.*

**Fanny**   Arrah Meelish! For the sake of that loving heart that is bleeding yonder, for the sake of those honest girls who stand bewildered at this charge against you, oh! for your own sake, speak out, say that no one has been concealed here! Raise up your face, girl, and say it is a lie.

*A pause.*

**All** (*murmuring*)   She doesn't spake! she doesn't spake!

**Fanny** (*after a pause, and when* **Feeny** *has disappeared*)   You desire, then, that all here should believe you guilty? You wish that Shaun should accept your silence as a confession of your shame?

**Shaun**  Fanny Power, if all Ireland thought her guilty; ay! if she said the word herself, and swore to it, I would not believe it agin' my own heart, that knows her too well to doubt her.

*Re-enter* **Feeny,** *and* **Soldiers** *and* **Sergeant.** *The two Soldiers who return with* **Feeny** *remain an the staircase – one on each side.*

**Feeny**  He has escaped; but here is his coat he left behind him; and look, here in the pocket is my pass that he stole.

**Arrah** *falls on her knees.*

**Major**  This evidence, Colonel, is pretty conclusive.

**O'Grady**  You see this, Arrah. (*Crossing to* **Arrah** *–* **Fanny** *steps back.*) Reflect, my good girl, that a cruel and painful death is the penalty of this crime.

**Arrah**  Take me away!

**O'Grady**  I believe that you are screening some unworthy villain at the cost of your own life. Speak, Arrah!

**Arrah** (*raising her arms*)  Take me away! Don't I offer my hands to the irons? Why don't you take me away?

**Shaun** (*rising*)  Stop! If she won't spake, I will. That coat there belongs to me.

**All the Peasants**  Shaun! (*A general movement of astonishment.*)

**Shaun**  I robbed Feeny of his money, and gave the notes to Arrah.

**Arrah**  Shaun! Shaun! what have you done?

**Arrah** *bursts from the Soldiers, and embraces* **Shaun.**

**Shaun**  I have trusted you. Hould up your head, my darlin'. (*Looks round.*) Who dar say a word agin ye now? Yes, O'Grady, put it all down to me, if ye plaze, sir. Don't cry, acuishla, sure they can't harm a hair of your head now.

**Arrah**  Oh, Shaun! what are you saying'? (*They handcuff* **Shaun** *between two Soldiers.*)

**Shaun**    Ye see how wrong ye all wor to be so hard upon her, and she as innocent as a child. Take her, Colonel dear, quick – asy! She has fainted, the crature. There, now, get me away handy before she's sinsible, the poor thing. Major dear, is it agin the regulations for me to take one kiss from her before I lave her, maybe for ever?

*He stoops over* **Arrah** *and embraces her.* **Shaun***'s hands are bound behind his back; two chains, fastened to the handcuffs, are each locked to the waistbelt of a Soldier, each side of* **Shaun***. As they take him off the Curtain falls.*

*End of Act One.*

# Act II

## Scene One

*The Devil's Glen.*

*Enter* **Beamish**.

**Beamish** What a night of adventure! I had a narrow escape from the barn, but favoured by the darkness I scaled the cliff, and stole away like a fox over the hills. What can detain Fanny? The hour appointed for our meeting has passed. Hark! some one comes down the glen. No; those are the footsteps of a man. 'Tis surely Oiny Farrell.

*Enter* **Oiny**.

**Oiny** Himself, yer honour, and it's the bad luck that's in it, sir, entirely.

**Beamish** What has happened?

**Oiny** Oh, the devil and all, sir – rade that while I get my breath. (*Hands him a letter.*)

**Beamish** It is from Fanny! Something has occurred to frustrate our plans. (*Reads.*) 'When I inform you that I have become acquainted with the relations subsisting between yourself and the person whose cabin you have lately inhabited, it will scarcely be necessary to add that we can never meet again!' Great heavens! what does this mean? (*Reads.*) 'I shudder when I think of you, so do not expose yourself to peril by attempting to see me. If any gentle feeling be awakened in your breast by the sad result of your crime, I appeal to that feeling to protect me from the insult of your presence – Fanny Power'.

**Oiny** It's thrue, indeed, sir! They found signs of yourself in Arrah's cabin. The girl wouldn't spake a word to let on who was in it, and when all the people was down upon her for the shame of the thing, sure Shaun stud up, and ses he, 'I am the man', ses he, and so he was tuk.

**Beamish**   What horrible porridge are you talking? Shaun arrested – for what?

**Oiny**   For robbing Feeny! Sure the notes was found in Arrah's pocket, and she wouldn't say how she come by them. Oh, but she stud it well.

**Beamish**   And this occurred after I left the barn?

**Oiny**   It did, sir.

**Beamish**   And was Miss Power present?

**Oiny**   Indeed she was, and she was mighty hard on Arrah, small blame on her! and all the neighbours was agin her, in regard to her desavin' Shaun.

**Beamish**   But why did you not tell the truth at once, and rescue the poor girl?

**Oiny**   Is it bethray yer honour?

**Beamish**   Do you mean that Shaun, to save me, has acknowledged to crimes that he never committed?

**Oiny**   Devil a ha'porth, sir; it was to save Arrah.

**Beamish**   He is ignorant, then, that I was the person concealed in the barn; for she promised me to keep my presence there a secret from him. He must believe the poor girl guilty.

**Oiny**   Well, it won't trouble him long, for they say the court-martial will be held on him today, and he'll be hung before mornin'.

**Beamish**   No. I will give myself up, and confess all.

**Oiny**   Confess that Arrah gave shelter to the outlaw? You would only shift the rope from his neck to hers.

**Beamish**   No – I think – at least, I hope no such unjust and inhuman sacrifice will be demanded. I will go at once to the Secretary of State at Dublin, and lay the whole history of my folly before him. Surely he will spare Arrah's life if I surrender mine.

**Oiny**   Ah! sure, sir, you wouldn't give yourself up?

**Beamish**   What object have I now in life? This cruel letter deprives me of defence and appeal. I know too well the promptitude of martial law. I have but a few hours to reach Dublin, obtain an audience, and to despatch the order from the authorities to suspend Shaun's execution. Meanwhile, return at once to Arrah, and tell her she has my leave to speak.

**Oiny**   She'd never do it, sir.

**Beamish**   Then let Shaun know the truth, and out with it.

**Oiny**   How can he, when it will convict his own girl?

**Beamish**   Then stand out yourself and proclaim these poor people to be innocent.

**Oiny**   Oh, iss! and how would I look? Faith I'd put myself in for it entirely. Sure I'd have to confess that I was through it all wid your honour.

**Beamish**   Then Fanny shall make the avowal. Yes, my confession will serve as the best answer to this letter, and she will understand my truth when I seal its utterance with my life. This evidence produced at the trial will save Shaun.

**Oiny**   But, sure I'll never be able to get back to Ballybetagh before the court-martial comes on.

**Beamish**   Follow me then, quickly. Oh, could I have foreseen that my wild adventure on Derrybawn would have had so unhappy a termination! Oh! Fanny, Fanny.

*Exit.*


## Scene Two

*The Armoury in* **O'Grady**'s *house.*

*The* **O'Grady** *and* **Major Coffin**.

**Major**   Really, Colonel, I cannot understand the grounds on which you profess to believe in the innocence of this fellow.

**O'Grady**   Sir, I have known him to be an honest man ever since he was a child.

**Major**   But he has confessed his guilt.

**O'Grady**   That is the only bad feature in the case.

**Major**   Bad feature! What evidence can be more conclusive? Don't you believe his word?

**O'Grady**   Egad, Major, if you think that he is capable of picking a pocket, won't you let me think him capable of telling a lie?

**Major**   The court-martial will decide that question. I am anxious to despatch this fellow's case at once, for the country is agitated, and prompt measures are required to restore order. It is my firm conviction that an example is particularly required at this moment to check a popular disturbance. This man's case admits of no doubt, and his execution will, I hope, prove a salutary public lesson. That being my firm conviction, Colonel, I trust you will excuse my prolonging any discussion upon the point. Good morning.

*Exit* **Major**.

**O'Grady**   There goes a kind-hearted gentleman, who would cut more throats on principle and firm conviction than another black-guard would sacrifice to the worst passions of his nature. If there be one thing that misleads a man more than another thing, it is having a firm conviction about anything.

*Enter* **Fanny Power**.

**Fanny**   You are quite right, I had a firm conviction. But if ever I have another – if ever I trust one of your sex again, may I be deceived, as I shall deserve to be!

**O'Grady**   What has happened?

**Fanny**   A change has come over me since last night. I am no longer the fool I was. I have learned a bitter lesson. Oh, may you never know what it is to be deceived by the being you love!

**O'Grady**   That will depend a good deal on yourself, my dear.

**Fanny**   May you never find the idol of your heart to be a worthless, treacherous, unfeeling thing, whose life is one long falsehood.

**O'Grady**   What is the matter with her?

**Fanny**   Oh! When I compare you with other men, how noble, how good you appear.

**O'Grady** (*aside*)   I wonder what I've been doing?

**Fanny**   And how base I feel when I reflect on the past.

**O'Grady**   Then don't reflect on it. Why should you remember it? Upon my word I'll forget it, with all my heart, whatever it is.

**Fanny**   Will you forgive me?

**O'Grady**   The man who hesitates to forgive a woman, under any circumstances, even when he hasn't the smallest notion of what she is talking about, deserves –

**Fanny**   That's enough – I ask no protestations – I have had over enough of them. Now to business, do you love me?

**O'Grady**   Ah, Fanny! I do, I do!

**Fanny**   You do. Oh, yes. I know too well that I have inspired you, and you only, with a true and faithful devotion – fool, fool that I have been!

**O'Grady**   I can't quite follow the process of reasoning by which you get to that result.

**Fanny**   There is my hand – you desire to make it yours. Well, it is yours on one condition.

**O'Grady**   I accept it, whatever it is.

**Fanny**   You must save the life of this poor fellow – Shaun' the Post – for I am in some measure the cause of his misfortunes.

**O'Grady**    You! What in the name of wonder can you have to do with his affair?

**Fanny**    Don't seek to learn more than is good for you to know. I was an accomplice in all this mischief, and the same bad influence, from which I have barely escaped with my life, has ruined Arrah Meelish.

**O'Grady**    But I would like to understand –

**Fanny**    Listen, then, for this much I may at least tell you. If I had not been deceiving you for the last two months; if I did not feel that I was unworthy of your love, and that I owe you some reparation for the suffering which I intended to inflict upon you, I would not say to you as I do now, 'O'Grady, I am yours'. (*Aside.*) Now, Beamish, farewell for ever. I have placed an impassable barrier between us, and – I am miserable for ever.

*Exit.*

**O'Grady**    I am bothered! She said 'I am yours'. But something within me, that feels like the conscience of my heart, refuses to send through every vein in my body those congratulations of delight that make a man feel conscious he is beloved. Woman! you were always the disturbing influence in the peaceful realms of human nature! Oh, Father Adam! Father Adam! Why didn't ye die with all your ribs in your body'?

*Exit.*

### Scene Three

*The Prison.*

**Shaun** *discovered.*

**Shaun**    Well, this is a sorry place for a man to spend his weddin' day in. It is not wid the iron cuffs on me, and wid a jug of could water for a companion, I expected to find myself this blessed night.

**Sergeant** *and* **Feeny** *appear at door, each with a lantern.*

**Sergeant**   The prisoner all right?

**Sentry**   All right, sir. (**Sergeant** *crosses to behind table.*)

**Shaun**   Who's that? It is Feeny, the dirty spalpeen, come to crow over my throuble. He shan't see that I am onaisy in my mind anyway.

**Shaun** *sings.*

**Feeny**   So it is singing ye are! as gay as a lark, eh? kapin up your sperits? That's right, my man, by-and-by you will be put on yer thrial, before the court martial.

**Shaun**   Well, to be sure! a court-martial itself. Is it in full jerrimentals they'll be?

**Sergeant**   Certainly. (*Crosses and goes out.*)

**Shaun**   And they won't charge me anything for seeing the show?

**Feeny**   They'll charge you with rebellion and robbery.

**Shaun**   And what'll they do to me for all that?

**Feeny**   You will be hung free of all expense – hung before tomorrow mornin' – that's the weddin' night you'll have. It's a wooden bride that is waiting for you, my jewel. It's only one arm she's got, and one leg, ho! ho! but, once she takes you round the neck, she's yours till death, ha! ha!

**Shaun**   And is hanging all they'll do to me?

**Feeny**   Nothing else, my dear.

**Shaun**   It's well it's no worse.

**Feeny**   Worse! What could be worse?

**Shaun** (*rising*)   They could make me a process-server, a polis spy, and a coward!

**Feeny** *crosses to behind table, passing behind* **Shaun**.

**Feeny**   Ho! you think to decave me wid your high sperits, but you don't! I know how you feel, wid the canker that's atin' your heart out. Sure, I loved Arrah, but I knew the bad dhrop was in her.

**Shaun**    It is well for you that I'm tied. Go on! go on!

**Feeny**    So don't be onaisy, she'll have somebody to comfort her afther you are gone, and that will be myself.

**Shaun**    Folly on! folly on!

**Feeny** *crosses back, keeping out of* **Shaun**'s *reach.*

**Feeny**    D'ye think I was decaved with the cloak you threw over her shame – not a ha'porth! She is guilty, and you know it as well as I do. You thought to save her by this schame; but, will I tell you what you have done? You have made her over to me as clane as if you had left her by will. Tomorrow, when you are over your trouble, I will show her the proofs I hould agin her, and she will be mine rather than face the disgrace of your death and the fear of her own.

**Shaun** (*breaks his chains with a cry of rage*)    Not when I can make sure of you first. Now, since the divil won't fetch ye, I'll send ye home. (*Seizing him by the throat, crams him down on his back on the table, and tries to strangle him.*)

**Feeny**    Help, Sergeant! he's loose! he is loose! (*The* **Sergeant**, *who has been speaking with the* **Sentry**, *seizes* **Shaun** *and forces him off* **Feeny**.) Hould him fast! have ye got him? Call the guard, till they skewer him agin the wall. (**Feeny**, *released, runs into corner.*) Isn't this purty tratement for an officer of the law in purshoot of his jooty? Oh, it is cryin' ye are, at last, Mr. Shaun. (*Circling in front round* **Shaun**, *who is helped up by* **Sergeant**, *and has flung himself on his seat at the table in a passion of grief.*) I thought your bright sperits would not last, ho! ho! (*The* **Sergeant** *takes him by the collar, and swings him to the door.*) Hollo!

**Sergeant**    Clear out! you mistake the place. This is a man in trouble, and not a badger in a hole to be baited by curs like you.

**Feeny**    I tell you what it is.

**Sergeant**  Sentry.

**Feeny**  I've got an ordther from your shupariors to visit the prisoner.

**Sergeant**  Put that man out. (*The* **Sentry** *takes him by the collar, and swings him out in a formal manner, recovers, salutes, faces about, and exit – the* **Sentry** *in going out is obliged to lower his musket to go out of door, and this action meets* **Feeny** *as he returns; he recoils before it, mistaking it for a menace.*)

**Feeny** (*returning at door*)  What am I going out for ? I've got an ord – (*Meets the bayonet of the* **Sentry**, *and disappears.* **Sergeant** *takes up* **Feeny**'s *hat between his fingers and throws it off, returns dusting his hands.*)

**Sergeant**  Come, prisoner, keep up your pluck, don't give way like a girl. This will never do – come, come, heads up, eyes right, you are not at the foot of the ladder yet.

**Shaun**  Oh! It's not what they can do to me that hurts me, but it is her sorrow that breaks my heart entirely.

*Enter* **Fanny Power**.

**Fanny**  There is an order from Major Coffin to admit me to see your prisoner. (*Hands* **Sergeant** *a paper.*) Tell me, Sergeant, as I entered I saw a girl sitting outside the prison gate, how long has she been there?

**Sergeant**  Well, miss, she has been lying there all night; the sentry warned her off and I told her that dogs and women was agin the regulations in barracks, but we didn't like to drive the poor thing away, as she promised to be quiet; so there she is.

**Fanny**  Leave us. (*Exit* **Sergeant**.) Shaun, you did not commit the crime of which you are self-accused, and rather than you shall suffer for the guilt of another, I will denounce the man I have loved, for 'twas he, my affianced husband, who was concealed in Arrah's cabin.

**Shaun**  And you believe he is false to you?

**Fanny**   Alas! I know it.

**Shaun** (*crosses to table*)   Thank ye kindly, miss; but I'd rather you'd hould your tongue about me, and let me die my own way, if you please.

**Fanny**   You believe, then, in Arrah's honesty?

**Shaun**   I never doubted her love for me.

**Fanny**   Poor, weak, blind, infatuated fool, you shall not sacrifice so truthful a heart to so bad an object. Shaun, the girl is outside now; will you see her?

**Shaun**   Will I see her? Would you ax a man dyin' of drooth if he'd have a drop of water?

**Fanny**   I'll set her face to face with him, and tax her with her guilt. I'll have it out.

*Opens door. Enter* **Sergeant**. **Fanny** *speaks to him, he shakes his head, she shows the pass, he reads, and they exeunt.*

**Shaun**   She's comin'! I'll see her again before I die. Now Shaun, mind me. Don't be showin' the sorrow in your breast, but comfort the poor crature you're going to leave behind ye, when you are dead and gone. Tuck in your sowl, ye poor, mane bodagh, and don't be showin' her the rags of your heart.

**Sergeant** *enters.* **Fanny** *leads in* **Arrah**, *then speaks to* **Sergeant** *aside, and they exeunt.* **Shaun** *does not see* **Arrah** *approaching him.*

**Arrah**   Shaun!

**Shaun**   Ar – Arrah!

**Arrah**   Shaun, don't ye – don't ye know your own wife?

**Shaun** (*embracing her*)   My wi – my own wife! Ah! say it again, for I darn't. (*They advance to front.*)

*Enter* **Fanny Power** *softly; she listens.*

**Arrah**   No, I won't; I did not mane to call myself by that name until you'd let me – until I had tould ye –

**Shaun**   Whisht, dear, what talk is that? There now, your eyes are heavy wid the tears in them, and you poor mouth it thrembles all over; don't spake about anything you don't like, acuishla.

**Arrah**   Oh, don't talk so softly to me, Shaun, for that hurts me. I have been decavin' you – I couldn't help it; but it's truth what they said. There was a young man concealed in the barn, and I am come to tell you who it was, an – an all about it (*sobs*) – if you'll only ax me, dear.

**Shaun**   Don't cry, darlin'; sure, I won't put any questions to you at all!

**Arrah**   Oh, but you must, dear, for d'ye think if I had not sworn to kape his secret, that I would have held my tongue last night, when, foreninst all the neighbours, your own wife was accused of bein' onthrue to ye? But I can't bear it any longer, Shaun, and sure he'd never hold me to a promise that made me look in your eyes the mane and guilty thing they call me, dear.

**Shaun**   It would be a great comfort entirely to myself, darlin', to feel that you had no sacrets from me, but you have made a promise, and you must kape your word, Arrah. You never broke it yet, and I won't ax you to begin now. (*Embrace.*) Sure when I'm dead I'll know all about it, but plaze God I'll die wid my faith in you entire, and no patches in it, my darlin'.

**Fanny** (*advancing*)   But no promise restrains me. The man concealed in your cabin was Beamish Mac Coul.

**Arrah**   Oh! Sure she has told!

**Shaun**   The Mac Coul! Oh, daylight to my sowl! The Mac Coul Himself ! Oh! bad luck to me for an omadhaun, and I never guessed it. Oh, Arrah, Arrah, don't think poorly of me for the joy that fills my heart; but wid the gallows before me, and not six hour maybe to live, I would not change that little ha'porth of time for any other hundred years of life, knowin' now as I know, and feelin' as I feel, that you are my own, that you love me, and me alone, always, now and for ever and ever. Amen.

**Fanny** (*aside*)   I begin to feel very uncomfortable. Have I made a fool of myself, after all?

**Shaun**   The Mac Coul himself! and he never let on to me that he was here in this place.

**Arrah**   It was for my sake, Shaun; he would not get ye in throuble.

**Shaun**   Oh, what did I do to deserve this of him, me that would go from the devil to Upper Canada to plaze the smallest hair of his head? Oh, wurrah, deelish, see this – it is too hard on me!

**Fanny**   Fool! ain't you going to die for him?

**Shaun**   Thrue for ye, miss. Well, that's some consolation, anyway. It's a proud man I'll be this day when I stand in the dock and Arrah to the fore looking at me, and saying 'It is Master Beamish himself would have been there if Shaun hadn't stud in his place.'

**Fanny**   It was not you, then, that robbed Feeny on Derrybawn?

**Shaun**   Me, miss – divil a ha'porth. Sure I see it all now – it was Mister Beamish himself he took the money to give to Arrah. He's as open-handed as ever – long life to him! – and if there's anythink cross about the way of it, why wouldn't I answer for it?

**Fanny**   Why did he not confess to me that he had found shelter in your cabin?

**Arrah**   Maybe he knew that you did not love him well enough to trust him, miss?

**Fanny**   Oh, what have I done! My word is passed to O'Grady! I feel as if I had committed suicide in a moment of temporary insanity. (*A drum is heard outside.*) Hark! they are coming to take Shaun before the court martial. What is to be done, Shaun, come what may, you must not die.

**Shaun**   Well, miss, to be sure. Life and Arrah is mighty sweet when taken together.

**Arrah**   Maybe he'll get off after all. They say the law is mighty unsartin.

**Fanny**   Unfortunately, Shaun has confessed he is guilty.

**Shaun**   Well, sure, now; if I confess I'm innocent, won't one go agin the other?

**Arrah**   No, I believe that they always take a man's word that he is a thief, but it's not worth a thrawneen to prove him an honest man.

**Fanny**   We must gain time – what defence can you make? If we could have got up an alibi.

**Shaun**   I've heern till that's a mighty fine thing entirely.

**Fanny**   But that is not to be thought of in your case.

**Arrah** (*aside to* **Shaun**)   What is it she is axin' for?

**Shaun**   I don't know rightly, jewil, but it's what lawyers always want when a man's in trouble. Have ye got ere an alibi, ses the judge. I have, ses the lawyer. That's enough, ses the court; dis-charge the prisoner.

**Fanny**   Listen; you must deny your guilt when they ask you whether you are guilty or not guilty.

**Arrah**   D'ye hear, Shaun?

**Shaun**   But I won't be makin' out anything agin the masther that way, will I, miss?

**Arrah**   Hould yer whist, and mind what you're bid.

**Fanny**   If they put any questions to you, avoid betraying yourself.

**Shaun**   Oh, never fear, I'm aquil to botherin' a regiment of the likes of them. I'll keep on saying nothing all the while. (*A drum outside.*)

**Sergeant** (*outside*)   Halt.

*Exit* **Fanny**.

*Enter* **Sergeant**, *and file of four Men. They unlock* **Shaun**'s *handcuffs.*

**Sergeant**   Halt! Sorry to interrupt you, but we must conduct the prisoner before the court-martial.

**Arrah**   Oh, Shaun, can't I go with you?

**Shaun**   No, my darling; but you get a good place in the court to see the show. Yes, miss, tell her – tell her I will get off. And tell him I'll hang with more to come pleasure for him. I'll get off, never fear. Tell her I'll get off. Good-bye, Anah, my heart goes with you. The sight of your face and the sound of your voice is the meat and drink of my soul. (*To* **Sergeant**, *who shakes his head – business to take Arrah off.*) Can't I go a little way with her? (*Advancing – business; he is led back.*)

**Sergeant**   Eh, prisoner, how's the courage, eh? Can I get you anything to get your heart up before the trial?

**Shaun**   Well, Sergeant dear, have ye such a thing about you as an alibi? or would ye borry it of a friend?

**Sergeant**   A halibi! Is it anything in the way of furrin' liquor?

**Shaun**   I don't know, but I thought you might.

**Sergeant**   I am afraid it's agin the regulations, for I never saw one in barracks. What quantity do you want?

**Shaun**   Egorra, that's a puzzler! Get me a whole one.

**Sergeant**   If it costs a month's pay you shall have it. Now, then, forward! Right about face – march!

**Shaun**   Don't you think I'll get off? Won't I, Sergeant, get off? (*Takes the arms of the two rear soldiers –* **Sergeant** *reproves him.*)

*Exeunt,* **Shaun** *in custody.*


## Scene Four

*Ballybetagh.*

*Enter* **Fanny**.

**Fanny** I would like to know what I could be guilty of now
to add to my folly and to my iniquity. By this time Beamish
must have received my letter. What will he do? Why he will
come here at once and deliver himself up. He will never permit
Shaun to suffer in his place. Then what will become of me?

*Enter* **Oiny**.

**Oiny** Long life t'ye, miss. Here's a bit of writin' that's in a hurry.

**Fanny** 'Tis from Beamish! (*Opens and reads.*) 'When you
receive this, I shall have surrendered to the authorities, My
avowal will exonerate Shaun, and my death will allay all fear
in your breast that you will ever again be insulted with the
presence of Beamish Mac Coul.' I knew it; I have driven him
to this. Where is he?

**Oiny** He's gone to inform on himself, miss. Sure, ses he, my
life is worth Shaun's and Arrah's put together. I'm off ses he.

**Fanny** Where to?

**Oiny** Well, to some grand man that dales in them things, I
believe, miss.

**Fanny** Oiny, go at once and order my horse to be harnessed
to the lightest vehicle in the O'Grady's stables.

**Oiny** That's the buggy, miss.

**Fanny** Give the horse a big feed, for a man's life is on his
speed tonight.

**Oiny** Then I'll wet his oats with a glass of whiskey, and he'll
fly, miss, never fear.

*Exit.*

**Fanny**   I have but one hope left. I must throw myself on
the generousity of the only man who can avert this terrible
catastrophe. He has granted a pardon to Beamish already; but
to be effective it must be unconditional. I must avow my folly to
him. I will appeal to his mercy – not for Beamish – but for my
wretched self. He can't refuse me; he won't; he shan't.

*Exit.*


## Scene Five

*The Justice Hall at Ballybetagh.*

*A row of seats slightly raised and oblique; a table opposite them; a barrier
across the back; a crowd of peasants,* **Oiny**, **Regan**, **Lanigan**, **Katty**
*etc;* **Feeny** *at the table; two clerks also at the table; the* **Sergeant**; *two
or three non-commissioned officers; soldiers on guard, and officers; a drum on
table; open doors at back;* **Colonol O'Grady**, **Major Coffin**, *and
three officers. As Scene draws, two Soldiers enter, and stand at entrances.*

**Sergeant**   Attention – shoulder arms – present – shoulder
arms – Order! Arms!

**Oiny**   Ah, d'ye see where you are scroogin' to ?

**Katty**   D'ye think there's nobody here but yourself?

**Lanigan** (*behind her*)   Mrs. Cooley, ma'am, would ye mind
takin' the back of your nightcap out of my mouth?

**Sergeant**   Order in the Court! Order!

**Katty**   Sergeant, dear, which is the Court, av ye plaze?

**Regan**   It's thim beyant in the goold lace.

**Lanigan**   Ah! go an – where's the wigs? (*Roll of the drum.*)

**Sergeant**   Attention! (*The Court sits.*)

**Major**   Sergeant, is everything prepared? Are we ready to try
the prisoner?

**O'Grady**   Let the prisoner be brought into Court.

**Sergeant** *goes out.*

*Enter* **Shaun** *between two Soldiers. Movement in the Court.*

**Regan**   Get out o' that, boys, and make room there for Arrah.

**Lanigan**   Stand back, Katty.

**Sergeant**   Order there!

**Katty**   Then hold your own whisht.

**Sergeant** *brings in* **Arrah**.

**Major**   Has the article of war constituting this court-martial been duly read? (**Sergeant** *bows.*) I think then, Colonel, we may proceed.

**Arrah** (*among the mob*)   Now mind what you are saying, darlin'.

**Shaun**   Never fear, dear, never fear – divil a ha'porth they'll get out of me.

**Major**   Your name?

**Shaun**   Is it my name, sir? Ah, you're jokin'! Sure there's his honour beside ye can answer for me, long life to him!

**Major**   Will you give the Court your name, fellow?

**Shaun**   Well, I'm not ashamed of it.

**O'Grady**   Come, Shaun, my man.

**Shaun**   There, didn't I tell ye! he knows me well enough.

**Major**   Shaun (*writing*), that's the Irish for John, I suppose.

**Shaun**   No, sir; John is the English for Shaun.

**Major**   What is your other name?

**Shaun**   My mother's name?

**Major**   Your other name.

**Shaun**   My other name? D'ye think I've taken anybody else's name? Did ye ever know me, boys, only as Shaun?

**All**  That's thrue. You may put that down agin him, Major.

**Sergeant**  Order!

**Regan**  What do you know about it?

**O'Grady**  He is called Shaun the Post.

**Shaun**  In regard of me carrying the letter – bag by the car, yer honour.

**Major**  Now, prisoner, are you guilty or not guilty?

**Shaun**  Sure, Major, I thought that was what we'd all come here to find out.

**Arrah**  Don't confess, Shaun.

**Shaun** (*aside*)  Never fear; I'm not such a fool as they think.

**Major** (*impatiently*)  Are you guilty or not guilty?

**Shaun**  How would I know till I hear the evidence?

**O'Grady**  Well, Shaun, you have pleaded guilty to this charge of robbery and violence.

**Shaun**  Well, O'Grady.

**Major**  Prisoner, you must not presume to address the Court with curt insolence, calling this gentleman 'O'Grady', in that familiar manner.

**O'Grady**  Your pardon, Major. You are not aware of our Irish way. I am O'Grady, the head of the sept. This man belongs to the sept of the Mac Coul, and as your kings are called without offence by their Christian names, 'George', or 'William', our chiefs are called 'O'Grady', or 'Mac Coul'. Pardon the digression – but the man gives me my title and no more. (**Major** *bows.*)

**Shaun**  Ah, the ignorance of thim Inglish!

**O'Grady**  Go on, my good man.

... pride guilty last night, and so I was thin, your worship; but I want to say that I am as innocent as a fish this morning.

**Major**  You wish to withdraw your plea?

**Shaun**  My what?

**Major**  Your plea.

**Shaun**  No – what would I ! (*Turning to crowd.*) Will I do that? (*They shake their heads.*) No, I couldn't, sir. (*The **Sergeant** leans over and whispers in **Shaun**'s ear.*) Oh, ah! Well – I see. I don't know, sir, but I want to do whatever will get me off.

**Major**  Withdraw his plea. The prisoner pleads 'Not Guilty'. (*Crowd shout.*)

**Shaun**  Thank ye kindly, Major. It is all over, Arrah. (*Jumps over dock* – **Sergeant** *expostulates with him.*)

**Major**  What is the fellow doing?

**Shaun**  Oh, Major, sure you wouldn't go back of your word. Didn't his honour say fair and plain – 'He is not guilty', ses he.

**All**  Oh, Major, ye did. Long life to the Major, boys.

**Sergeant**  Order there. (*The **Sergeant** forces **Shaun** back into the dock.*)

**Shaun**  You can't thry a man twice over for the same offinse.

**Major**  Really this must be stopped; the dignity of the court must be preserved.

**Shaun** (*to the crowd*)  D'ye hear that, boys? Preserve your dignity, you blackguards, till ye get outside.

**Major**  Now, Mr. Feeny, state your charge.

**Feeny** (*rising*)  Plase your worships. (*Advances to the end of table.*) (*Jeers from crowd.*)

**O'Grady**  Stop. What's your name?

**Feeny**   Michael Feeny.

**O'Grady**   Your business?

**Feeny**   Well, your worship –

**O'Grady**   Don't worship me, man, and confound me in your mind with the devil. Speak straight, if you can. What's your dirty trade?

**Feeny**   Sure ye know well enough, sir. I am an officer of the law, sir.

**O'Grady**   I do know you well enough, but these gentlemen do not, and I mean they shall. Are you a process-server?

**Feeny**   Well?

**O'Grady**   Yes or no?

**Feeny**   Y-e-e-es.

**O'Grady**   An informer on occasions?

**Feeny**   I did –

**O'Grady**   Out with it! – yes or no.

**Feeny**   Y – yes.

**O'Grady**   How many times have you been committed to gaol?

**Feeny**   Is it me that's on my thrial, Colonel, or Shaun the Post?

**O'Grady**   Don't question me, sir. I want an answer. Come, how often were you in prison?

**Feeny**   I disremember.

**Crowd** (*jeering*)   He disremembers!

**O'Grady**   No doubt, but I don't. (*Takes up a paper and reads.*) Three times for perjury, once for theft, and three times for petty offences. (*Looks up.*) Will I name the prisons and the length of your periods of incarceration?

**Feeny** I wouldn't ax –

**O'Grady** Yes or no?

**Feeny** (*quickly*) No. (*A laugh in the Court.*)

**O'Grady** Now, go on; the Court has your name and trade; you may proceed –

**Feeny** (*whimpering*) It's mighty hard, so it is, to be put upon this way, and me only doing my duty. Sure your worships knows well all I've got to say. It's tuk down in the impositions agin the prisoner. Is it my fault if Shaun confessed to the robbery? Did I put the idays in his head or the notes in his pocket? Then why am I to be schraped down to bethray my misfortunes underneath? It's mighty hard upon me entirely, so it is.

**O'Grady** You come here to accuse the prisoner; stop snivelling over yourself, and thry your hand on him.

**Feeny** Sure, Colonel, dear, Shaun has accused himself.

**Major** Do you swear that the notes produced were part of the property of which you were robbed?

**Oiny** Now isn't that a quare question for the Major to ask? – a fellow that would swear the bark out of an old dog! (*Jeers and menaces.*)

**Feeny** I do, sir.

**Major** Prisoner, do you wish to ask this witness any questions?

**Shaun** I wouldn't bemane myself by bein' seen talkin' to him.

**All** Long life to you, Shaun!

**Major** Stand down.

**Feeny** *retires.*

**Katty** Oh! look at him, sitting on the size of a sixpence!

**Oiny**   Look at his whisker! – like a dirty ha'porth of tobacco!

**Major**   You hear what he says – if these notes were his, how came they in your possession?

**Shaun**   Sure, Major, that's what he didn't prove – he broke down there entirely, sir.

**Major**   But this is for you to establish.

**Shaun**   Sure, Major that would be accusing myself.

**Major**   Have you heard the evidence?

**Shaun**   Do you call that evidence? Yes, I did – I heard all of it; and if I am to be found guilty on that chap's swearin', it will be a wrong bill. The Recordher knows him well, and wouldn't sintence a flay for backbitin' on that fellow's oath. Come out of that, Michael Feeny, and hear me. When St. Pathrick drove all the crapin' things out of Ireland, he left one sarpint behind, and that was your great grandfather.

**Major**   This is not to the point.

**O'Grady**   It is a mighty fine outburst of natural eloquence; go on, my man, crush that reptile if you can.

**Shaun**   Crush him. I'd ax no better. I've had him under my fist; but he is like some vermin ye can't crush, they stick so flat in the dirt.

**Major**   This is very irrelevant.

**O'Grady**   That's prejudice, Major. I never listened to anything more compact in the way of vituperation.

**Major**   But abuse is not evidence. (*To* **Shaun**.) Have you any witnesses to call?

**Shaun**   Devil a one, Major, barin' you'd like to stand up for a poor boy in throuble yourself, and say a good word for me.

**Major**   Then this case is closed. I think, gentlemen the facts are plain. We have but one duty to perform.

**O'Grady**   I'm for letting him off.

**Major**   On what grounds?

**O'Grady**   The eloquence of the defence.

**Major**   I regret to say that we cannot admit so Irish a consideration.

**O'Grady**   Well, gentlemen, I have private reasons for believing this man to be innocent, and you will oblige me in a particular manner if you believe so too.

**Major**   In defiance of your convictions, Colonel?

**O'Grady**   That will only add to obligation, Major. I have given my word to a lady that I would get this fellow off.

**Major**   Do you consider, sir, the debt of duty we owe your sovereign?

**O'Grady**   I do sir but a premise made to a lady is a debt of honour, and that is always paid before taxes.

**Major**   Gentlemen, your voices –

**Arrah**   Oh, the pain that it is in my heart.

*A pause, after which the Court reseats.*

**Major**   Prisoner, the Court having considered the evidence against you, and having duly weighed the matters alleged by you in defence, declares the charge made against you of associating and conspiring with rebels in arms against the peace of His Majesty and the realm; and also of robbery with violence, done on the person of Michael Feeny, to be fully proven, and of the felonies aforesaid you are found guilty.

**All**   Guilty! Poor Shaun! Oh, blessed day! Oh, murder! What'll be done to him?

**Arrah**   Shaun. (*Throws herself into his arms.*)

**O'Grady**   I'm sorry for you, Shaun. I would have let you off if a minority of one against four would have done it; but you see we are unanimous against you, my poor boy, so whether you committed the crimes or not, you are guilty. It's mighty hard upon you to say so.

**Major**   Colonel, permit me to remark that these observations coming from the Court are subversive of its dignity.

**O'Grady**   Ah, Major, look at that poor girl that lies broken-hearted on the body of the man she loves, knowing that there's not a day's life in the breast she's clinging to. It is a hard duty that obliges a gentleman to put a rope round that boy's neck, while dignity forbids him to say that he's mighty sorry for it. (*Rises and quits the room, the Officers rise and bow, and reseat themselves.*)

**Major**   Prisoner, we deeply regret the sentence which it is incumbent upon us to pass upon you; but the Court knows only its duty and the penalty ascribed to your crime. The sentence of the Court is – (*the Officers remove their hats*) – that you be taken hence to your prison from whence you came, and tomorrow at daylight, you suffer death, and Heaven have mercy upon you! (*The Officers replace their hats.*)

**Shaun**   Well, yer honour, I don't blame ye, for you have done your jooty, I suppose, by the King that made ye what ye are – long life to him! – and that jooty is now to hang me; and I have done my duty by the man that made me and mine what we are, and that's to die for him. I could do no more, and you could do no less. I dare say you would have let me off if you could, so God bless ye, all the same.

**Major**   Remove the prisoner.

*Murmurs among the crowd getting louder. They break through barrier, seize* **Michael Feeny**, *and after severe struggle with soldiers, throw him violently to the ground.* **Arrah** *fainting,* **Shaun** *guarded, as Act-drop descends.*

*End of Act Two.*

# *Act III*

## Scene One

*A room in Dublin Castle; a fireplace with screen; a table, with papers and shaded light, chairs, etc, a bay-window, curtained; a door.*

**Winterbottom**, *asleep in the chair before the fire. A knock.*

**Winterbottom** (*awaking*)   Hi was under the happreension I 'erd a knock. (*A knock.*) That's him.

*Enter the* **Secretary**.

**Secretary**   I am a little late, I think, Winterbottom. My dressing-gown? (*Throws off his coat – puts on his dressing-gown.*) Now for work. You will come to me as usual at midnight, and rouse me to go to bed. (*Sits at table examining letters, and writes.*)

**Winterbottom**   Can I do hanything helse for your lordship?

**Secretary**   Nothing. Good night!

**Winterbottom**   Good night, my lord. Ho! I forgot, there's a young gentleman, a perfect gentleman, 'as been a-waiting below since six o'clock.

**Secretary**   Who is he? did he give you his name?

**Winterbottom**   No, my lord.

**Secretary**   Then how did you know he was a perfect gentleman?

**Winterbottom**   He give me a fi'pun' note, my lord.

**Secretary**   I beg your pardon. Show that perfect gentleman here. (*Exit* **Winterbottom**, *carrying the* **Secretary***'s coat.*) These disturbances in Wicklow threaten to involve us once more in endless trouble. Could we discover the ringleaders of the movement, we might arrest its progress, but all our efforts to detect them seem fruitless.

*Re-enter* **Winterbottom**, *ushering in* **Beamish Mac Coul**, *the* **Secretary** *rises; they bow.*

**Winterbottom**   Shall I wait, my lord, or –

**Secretary**   No, you can go to bed.

**Winterbottom**   Werry good, my lord. (*Bows and exit.*)

**Secretary**   I regret, sir, to have kept you so long in waiting. Will you favour me with your name, and in what manner I can be of service to you? I pray you to be seated. (*Sits behind table.*)

**Beamish** (*by table*)   My name, my lord, is Beamish Mac Coul, and I come to place my person at the disposition of the Crown.

**Secretary**   Beamish Mac Coul – you!

**Beamish**   It is true, and I rely on your forbearance to listen kindly to my apology. For six weeks past I have been organizing an insurrection in the mountain districts of Wicklow; I saw enough to prove that our designs would be – a useless waste of life, therefore our plans were abandoned, and I had resolved to return to France this day.

**Secretary**   A very prudent resolution: I regret you have not adhered to it.

**Beamish**   Here, my lord, is a confession of my participation in this affair. One of my-former tenants has been arrested, tried, and by this time has, doubtless, been found guilty, on his own confession, of the acts which I committed, and of which he is totally innocent.

**Secretary**   Wherefore has this fellow confessed?

**Beamish**   That he might bear the penalty of my crime, while I escaped.

**Secretary**   And you come here to claim his release and your own execution?

**Beamish**   If you please, my lord.

**Secretary**   I presume, then, that you and this fellow are disputing which of the two shall die?

**Beamish**  And I rely on your lordship's sense of justice to give me the preference.

**Secretary** (*rises and walks to the fire*)  Shall I ever be able to understand this extraordinary people? (*A knock.*) What new disturbance comes at this untimely hour? My poor Winterbottom can scarcely have gained his bed.

**Winterbottom** (*half dressed*)  A gentleman on horseback, my lord.

**Secretary**  Is he a perfect gentleman?

**Winterbottom**  I can't say, my lord. He only give me his card. (*Handing it in.*) Hexcuse me, my lord, but in my 'aiste I hain't quite in the condition I should wish to appear.

**Secretary** (*takes card and reads – aside*)  Colonel O'Grady. Ha, indeed; show the gentleman here at once. (**Winterbottom** *at once disappears.*) Will you withdraw into the recess of yonder window, for this interview, I think, concerns you?

**Beamish**  I consider myself a Crown prisoner, and am at your lordship's disposal. (*Retires behind curtain of window.*)

**Secretary**  So, Colonel O'Grady, you applied for and obtained this young gentleman's pardon at the very moment when he was provoking a sedition, and for which you were about to bestow upon him the hand of your ward.

*Enter* **Winterbottom***, showing in the* **O'Grady***.*

**Secretary**  Your servant, Colonel.

**Winterbottom**  Shall I wait hup, my lord?

**Secretary**  By no means. You will get no rest at all.

**Winterbottom**  No Hinglishman hexpects hanny, my lord, in this country. It keeps us hall hup, and continually deprives Hingland of her natural rest. (*Aside.*) I 'ope the gentleman will take the 'int.

*Exit.*

**Secretary**    Now, Colonel, I am at your service. (*Sits.*)

**O'Grady**    I know your lordship will pardon this untimely intrusion when you learn that the sentence of death will in a few hours be executed on a man who is –

**Secretary**    As innocent as you are of the acts of which he is accused. (*Reading.*) Let me see. His name is Shaun the Post, residing at Rathdrum.

**O'Grady**    You astonish me – how could this intelligence have reached you? I left the court martial a few hours ago, and spurred across the country as fast as my horse could carry me.

**Secretary**    My dear Colonel, the Government sources of information are much more extraordinary than we care to acknowledge. We have all the particulars of the matter.

**O'Grady**    I am glad to see you share my conviction that this fellow is not guilty.

**Secretary**    He is not! I know the real culprit.

**O'Grady**    The devil you do!

**Secretary**    Allow me to enjoy your confusion.

**O'Grady**    Will you allow me to enjoy a little of it also, for hang me if I know who you mean.

**Secretary**    His name is Beamish Mac Coul.

**O'Grady**    The devil! A thousand pardons; but would you say that again?

**Secretary**    Come, Colonel, your surprise is admirably assumed! but since you carry it so far, I must inform you that the Government sources of information even extend to occurrences in your own household. (*Looking over paper.*) Six weeks ago Beamish Mac Coul landed in Wicklow (*Colonel rises*) coming from France, with the design of marrying your ward, Miss Fanny Power of Cabinteely, to whom he has for many years been ardently attached. You see, Colonel, disguise is useless. Your little family matters are well known to the Privy Council.

**O'Grady**   By the Lord Harry! the Council then is privy to more of my family matters than I am at all acquainted with (*A knock.*)

**Secretary**   Another attack on poor Winterbottom. (*Rises.*) Who can this be?

**O'Grady**   My lord, allow me to inform you that the lady in question is my affianced wife. I hope you will excuse me if I accord more confidence to my sources of information on this point than to any on which your Government may rely.

**Secretary** (*aside*)   His affianced wife! (*Aloud.*) Then, why, Colonel, have you so ardently sought this young man's pardon?

**O'Grady**   Because Fanny demanded it.

**Winterbottom** (*in a night cap; puts his hand in at door*)   A lady in a buggy, my lord.

**Secretary**   Are you sure, Winterbottom, that it is a lady?

**Winterbottom**   Quite sure, my lord. She wouldn't take no for a hanswer. She was werry 'igh indeed with the 'all porter, and she 'anded me two notes – this one for your lordship. (*Gives in a letter.*)

**Secretary** (*reads it*)   Oh indeed. I will see the lady immediately.

**Winterbottom**   Yes, my lord.

*Exit.*

**Secretary**   I regret, Colonel, to defer your business for a few moments. Would you take this chair by the fire, while I give audience to that fair intruder; and I hope to be able to convince you, sooner perhaps than you suspect, how perfect is our detective system of police. (**O'Grady** *sits behind screen.*)

*Re-enter* **Winterbottom**, *dressed, and bearing the* **Secretary**'s *coat, which he assists him to put on.*

**Secretary** (*reads card*)   Miss Fanny Power, of Cabinteely. So now I perceive the drift of this business. Young Mac Coul was evidently an old sweetheart of this girl. In his absence she takes up with the O'Grady. He returns to claim her hand, and the crafty minx obtains, through lover No. 2, the pardon of her old flame, with which she pays off his prior claim. A very neat female transaction! (**Winterbottom** *bows in* **Fanny Power**. *Exit with dressing-gown, concealing it from* **Fanny**'s *sight as he bows himself out, handing her to a seat.*) To what good fortune may I attribute this favour?

**Fanny** (*throwing back her mantle*)   Oh, my lord, it is ill-fortune brings me to your feet.

**Beamish** (*looking out*)   Fanny!

**O'Grady** (*turning to listen*)   Powdhers of war! what's that?

**Fanny**   Pardon my agitation, but now that I find myself in your presence, I have lost the courage that sustained me, and perceive only the shame of my proceedings.

**Secretary**   Compose your feelings while I assist you to put in due order the favours you have resolved to obtain from me. First, you will ask me for a remission of the sentence of Shaun the Post, now left for execution for a felony committed by Beamish Mac Coul.

**Fanny**   By what power can you read my thoughts?

**Secretary**   Ahem! my dear young lady, the sources of information at the command of His Majesty's Government are extraordinary.

**Fanny**   Then you know that for many a happy year I have corresponded with the outlaw (**O'Grady** *turns*) – that he returned from his exile, invited by and relying upon my love.

**Secretary**   But meanwhile a certain gallant colonel had won your affections away from the absentee, and as you have lately become the affianced wife of this gentleman, you desired, in lieu of your hand, to recompense your discarded lover with a full pardon.

**Fanny**   I am afraid the sources of information of His Mayesty's Government fail when they try to investigate a

Mac Coul with a deeper passion since I wronged him by suspicion, and I became irrevocably his from the moment I gave myself to another.

**O'Grady** (*falling back in his chair*)   Oh, Fanny!

**Secretary** (*aside*)   Ahem! What an awkward disclosure! (*Rises.*) I don't quite understand.

**Fanny** (*rises*)   I have deceived these two gentlemen, who love me with all their honest hearts, and how have I requited them? I enticed Beamish to return to this country, to the foot of the scaffold, and then, in a moment of anger, I cast him off and bestowed my worthless self on the O'Grady.

**Secretary**   Whereupon the young rebel surrendered himself, and is now a Crown prisoner. Under the circumstances you allege, you must pardon me if I speak in the language your future husband would employ if he were here and could exercise the powers I hold. The surrender of this hot-headed young man is only known to me. Let him return at once to his exile, and pledge his word never again to set foot in this country. On these conditions he is free to depart.

**Fanny**   He will do so – he will. He is not so cruel as I am. He will not sacrifice his life, as I have done, to be revenged upon his love.

**Secretary** (*withdrawing the curtain*)   Let him answer for himself.

**Fanny**   Beamish!

**Beamish**   I have heard your confession, and (*to* **Secretary**) I accept your lordship's generous offer; for your sake, Miss Power, I accept it. I yield to one who loves you sincerely, and who deserves you far better than I do. You have wronged him – tell him so. He is generous enough to love you none the less for it. Farewell!

**Fanny**   Can you – will you ever forgive me?

**Beamish** (*advances to table*)   My exile, which hitherto has been my sole regret, now becomes my only consolation; for when thus separated from you, I shall feel entitled to indulge that love which absence never has enfeebled and time can never efface. Farewell for ever!

**Fanny**   Oh, Beamish, do not part from me in this cruel manner. Will you not give me your hand? What! not even a look? Do you think O'Grady would blame you if at such a moment you bestowed on me one poor embrace?

**O'Grady** (*kicking over the screen*)   No! I'll be hanged if he would! Look you, my lord, what d'ye take me for? You would make me serve a writ of ejectment on my rival, that I may enjoy his property in this lady. Stop – stop! till I pull myself together, and recover my saddle. Oh, Fanny, Fanny! Damme, my lord, I'll fight him for it, if you like; but when you ask me to take legal means of righting myself, you forget I am an Irishgentleman, and not a process-server!

**Fanny**   Oh, now I'm ruined entirely!

**Secretary**   I seem to have conducted this affair to a successful eruption.

**O'Grady**   Don't you know that the woman that marries one man – when she loves another commits bigamy, with malice prepense? What harm did I ever do you, that you should contemplate making a tombstone of me to remind you of that young gentleman!

**Fanny**   I am a mass of iniquity. I don't know what is to be done with me.

**O'Grady**   Yes, you do; you know well enough you will become Mrs. Beamish Mac Coul, if his lordship will only give you the chance; and if the Government feels, as he says, under any slight obligations to me, they will requite them if they will enable you to make that gentleman half as miserable as you have made me.

behaviour?

**O'Grady**  I'll be one.

**Fanny**  I'll be the other. I'll secure him.

**Beamish**  How shall I express my acknowledgments in language –

**O'Grady**  Oh! (*Striking his forehead, and then running to look for his hat and whip.*) The divil admire me – I forgot Shaun. Here we are exchanging the height of politeness while we left him beside the door of death, and it only on a jar. (*Looks at his watch.*) I've only got two hours and six minutes to cover thirty miles.

**Fanny**  Here's your hat!

**O'Grady**  It's not that I want so much as me whip.

**Secretary**  Shall I despatch a courier to arrest proceedings? (*Rings bell and writes at table.*)

**O'Grady**  Give it to me. I know what Government speed is. If any animal can get over the ground in time to save the boy (*receives paper*) – I am that individual. So, my lord, pardon the disordher of my leave-taking, and the hasty expression of my acknowledgments.

*Enter* **Winterbottom**.

**O'Grady**  Now, Mr. Summerbottom, show me the door.

*The Scene closes in as* **O'Grady** *goes out and* **Fanny** *and* **Beamish** *are taking leave of the* **Secretary**.


**Scene Two**

*Ballybetagh – Moonlight.*

*Enter* **Regan**, **Oiny**, **Moran**, **Lanigan**.

**Regan**  Not a sign of anybody comin' from Dublin.

**Oiny**   And them military wouldn't sthretch an hour though they knew a minute itself would save them.

*Enter* **Patsey**.

**Oiny**   Well, Patsey, is there a good word in your mouth?

**Patsey**   Oh, murdther, boys, but it's no use; his place is tuk be the car that never comes back. He is lyin' beyant in the cell there, whereye see the light. Divil a soul is let near him, only the priest.

**Oiny**   Isn't Arrah wid him?

**Patsey**   Not a bit of her; she's keenin round the place like a bewildered sheep, and they keepin' her off wid their bagginets.

**Lanigan** *and* **Regan**   Ah! the poor creature.

**Oiny**   That's the way'of it. Divil a consolation they'll let him have, only bread and wather for tay, and the sound of the clock for company.

**Patsey**   I'd give half of my life to save Shaun.

**Oiny**   The half you're done wid, I suppose.

**Patsey**   Couldn't someone get up by some manes to his windy outside there?

**Oiny**   Ah, Baithershin, is it up the face of the cliff! D'ye think you're a fly, and can walk on nothing?

**Regan**   Not a human crature could rache that, barrin' he was a saygull.

**Patsey**   Well, then, sure, I know where the gunpowdher is stored in the vaults below the Castle. Wouldn't it be easy to blow the place to smithereens?

**Regan**, **Lanigan** *and* **Moran**   Oh; that's fine! that ud astonish them.

**Oiny**   Iss' and it would take a rise out of Shaun, be the same token.

**Patsey**   Oh be japers! I never thought o' that.

spade is ready for him; and if help doesn't come from Dublin in time, he is past prayin' for. Let us go and say a soft word to Arrah. Where will we find the poor thing?

**Patsey**   I saw her just now climbin' the Castle-hill there, to get on the battlements above Shaun's cell, to be as near him as she cud.

**Oiny**   Ah, then let her alone. Her sorrow is as wide and deep as the salt say. It would be only foolish for ourselves to thry and dhraw it off wid a bucket.

*Exeunt.*

## Scene Three

*The Prison.*

**Shaun** *discovered with the* **Priest** *at a table.*

**Shaun**   It's thrue for your rivarence. I know, sir, that I have only a couple of hours to live, and I ought to be listenin' and mindin' what you say, and turnin' my sowl to its prospects. But my heart is too sthrong for me, and I can't hould it back from thinkin' of the poor darlin' girl I'm lavin' behind me. But go on, sir; I'll thry to to attend, an' make meself fit to die. Iss, sir, now I'm listenin', I won't think of her for ten whole minutes. (*The* **Priest** *draws the candle to him, and is about to read –* **Shaun** *looks up.*) Didn't ye say you saw her standin' outside the prison-gate, as you come in' ? Poor crature – outside – iss – think o' that I think I see her hungry eyes look through the bars. Bless her! Ah! I forgot, sir; I ax your pardon, sir; I won't do it agin! Now I'm – I'm – not thinkin' of her. (*The* **Priest** *is going to recommence.*)

*Enter the* **Sergeant** *–* **Shaun** *runs to him.*

**Shaun**   Ah! Sergeant, did you see her? Where is she?

**Sergeant**   Yes; I saw her.

**Shaun**    Oh! Sergeant, dear. What a happy man you are. Ah! if I could have given you my eyes. You saw her, and where is she at all?

**Sergeant**    She is sitting on the Watch Tower, just above here.

**Shaun**    Above our heads! Is it my darlin' is up there, or maybe she'd be more this way to the corner? Eh! Sergeant? Ah! tell me – tell me where she is, that I may look to the spot, and fix the lips of my heart upon it.

**Sergeant**    If that window were not closed with iron bars, you might see her; for her eyes are fixed on it. She's just over that corner of your cell.

**Shaun**    High up; on the top of the Castle, where it joins the cliff. I know the place. And did you spake to her?

**Sergeant**    I did, as well as I could. Her tears fell faster than I could wipe them away with my handerkercher (*draws it out*) – and I'd enough to do to cry halt to my own.

**Shaun** (*taking his handkerchief away as he was going to dry his eyes with it*)    Are her tears in this? See how mine come out to look at them! (*Kisses it.*) Sergeant, when I die you'll put this round my eyes, won't ye'? (*Puts it in his breast.*) And did she spake t'ye?

**Sergeant**    Yes; she said 'Sergeant, would you ordher a fire to be lighted in Shaun's cell?'

**Shaun**    A fire! Sure it is not cowld.

**Sergeant**    So I replied; but she only repeated the same words, and I promised I would have it done.

*Enter two Soldiers with fuel. They go to the open hearth and make a fire.*

**Shaun**    Ah, my poor Arrah! I know what she wants. Sure won't she see the smoke comin' from the chimbly above, and she will know it comes from where I am. Ah, your riverance, don't ax me to think of anything else for a while. In another hour will ye see me again, and thin my heart will be broken entirely, and ye can do wid me what ye will. (*Sits down.*)

*Exit the* **Priest**.

**Sergeant**    There now, I will leave you for half an hour; but if you feel lonely, I shall be in the guard-room. Kick at the door yonder, and the sentry will pass the word for me.

**Shaun**    Ah, Sergeant, but the milk of a good nature is as new in your heart this minute as when you firrst dhrew woman's kindness from your mother's breast.

**Sergeant** (*shaking his hand*)    If I am obliged to refuse your girl admission to see you, don't blame me, Shaun. It is my duty, and the reg'lation, you know.

**Shaun**    Av coorse it's your jooty; you can't help it. I would do the same if I was in your place, and make you a corporal. (*Exit* **Sergeant**.) That's'a lie, but no matter; it will be a comfort to him to think so. Ah! now I can look at her: there she is this minute. I can hear the beating of her heart. No; it's my own, I hear. Well, it's all the same Oh, Arrah, jewel, if you could hear me; if – (*a stone and letter fall down the chimney*) What's that? (*Runs and picks it up.*) A stone, and a bit of paper rowl'd round it – 'tis from her – from herself – there's writin' on it. Oh, that's why she wanted me to have a fire – ho! ho! he! God bless her! think o' that. Ah! the cunnin' of the crature! (*Kisses the paper.*) Oh, murdher, what am I about? Maybe I'd rub it out. Now let me read. What the divil's got in my eye? (*He cries, and wipes his eyes with the* **Sergeant**'s *handkerchief.*) There, now there, haven't you tears done kissin' one another yet? (*Reads.*) 'My darlin', I am near by you. Oh, but my eyes is hungry for you, Shaun. I'm lookin' down to where you are now radin' this. I'm stretchin' my arms towards ye. Oh! Shaun, God bless ye, and may He help you to find the heaven that I have lost in this world'. Oh, Arrah, me heart is brakin' entirely. (**Arrah** *is heard above, and at a distance singing.*) Whisht – 'tis herself – she's thryin' to let me know that she is there. (*He draws the table to the window, and clings to the bar as he listens.*) She's there – she's there – she calls to me, and I'm caged. Arrah! Arrah! I can't rache ye; I can't kiss away your tears, and howld ye to my heart. Oh! the curse of

Crumwell on these stones. Eh, the iron moves under my hand: the bars are loose in their sockut. Whisht – no – it's the stone itself that's split. Oh, murther, could I push it out? It's goin': by jakers it's gone. Whisht! I hear it thundering down the wall. Splash – it's in the waves below – it is a hundred feet clane fall. (**Arrah** *repeats her song.*) She's callin' me agin. I'll go to her. (*Throws off his coat.*) The wall is ould and full of cracks; the ivy grows agin it. It is death, maybe, but I'll die in sthrivin' to rache my girl, and chate the gallows that's waitin' for me. She's on the road to heaven, anyway; and if I fall, may the kind angels that lift up my sowl, stop for one minute as they pass the place where she is waitin' for me, till I see her once agin. (*He escapes through the window.*)

*The scene changes to the exterior of the same tower; the outside of the cell is seen, and the window by which he has just escaped.* **Shaun** *is seen clinging to the face of the wall; he climbs the ivy. The tower sinks as he climbs; the guardroom windows lighted within are seen descending, and above them a rampart, and* **Sentry** *on guard. Chorus of soldiers inside guardroom. As* **Shaun** *climbs past the window, the ivy above his head gives way, and a large mass falls, carrying him with it; the leaves and matted branches cover him. His descent is checked by some roots of the ivy, which hold fast. An alarm. The* **Sentry** *advances and looks over rampart into the abyss; the curtains of the guardroom window are withdrawn; the* **Sergeant**, *with candle and five Soldiers put out their heads.*

**Sentry**  Who goes there? (*Distant alarms – a pause.* **Arrah**'s *song repeats above.*)

**Sergeant**  It's all right. Tis only that girl above there – has displaced some of the masonry. (*Withdraws with the Soldiers; the curtains are replaced.*)

**Sentry**  All's well!

**Several Sentries in the distance**  All's well! All's well!

**Arrah**'s *song continues. The ivy moves, and* **Shaun**'s *head appears amongst it; he emerges, and continues his ascent; he eludes the* **Sentry**, *and disappears round the corner of the tower, still ascending. The scene still* *descends, showing the several stages of the keep, until it sinks to the platform, in which* **Arrah** *is discovered seated and leaning over the abyss, still singing the song. Beyond, there is seen the lake and the tops of the Castle.*

*Enter* **Feeny**.

**Feeny**    There she is! I thought I heern her keenin and howlin'. Arrah! jewel, listen to me. It's all over wid Shaun. Salt-pether wouldn't save him. And the whole country is up in arms agin you and me.

**Arrah** (*rocking herself*)    What is the whole country, or the whole world, to me now? Oh! achone!

**Feeny**    They say that Shaun is dying to save your character, and you have let him do it. The place will be too hot to howld ye, or me aither. Let us lave it entirely, and if you'll put up wid me, I'll help ye to forget Shaun.

**Arrah**    Michael Feeny, I'd rather take the man that puts my boy to death this comin' momin' than have you, if you were rowlin' in goold and dimins. Is that enough for you?

**Feeny**    Will nothin' bend your heart? (*Goes up to her.*)

**Arrah**    Nothin'! it will break first.

**Feeny**    What's that noise there'? (*Advances, looks over.*) Whisht. Something is moovin' over the face of the wall – there below. It's a man climbin' to this – Oh! Arrah, come here – come quick. Oh, your heart will break rather than bend or stoop to me! then it shall break: look down there. D'ye see that form below clingin' to the ivy, and crawlin' slowly towards this spot? Does your heart tell ye who it is?

**Arrah**    Ah!

**Feeny**    Tis Shaun! Shaun, that your voice is drawin' up to your side-crawlin' through the jaws of death.

**Arrah** (*falling on her knees as she looks*)    Oh, my darlin' – Oh, my dear.

**Feeny**  Will I give the alarm? A bullet from the senthry would send him to glory wid one plunge, or this stone would pick him off.

**Arrah**  No! (*Clings to him.*)

**Feeny**  I tould ye my time would come when I'd make you feel the sorro ye haped on me.

**Arrah**  Let me – let me spake t'ye.

**Feeny**  Not a word but one. Will ye be mine? (*Seizes the stone.*)

**Arrah**  Would ye murther him?

**Feeny**  It's no murther; but anybody's right to kill the condemned felon escaping from his sentence. Spake out, and answer.

**Arrah**  Must I take ye, or see him killed under my eyes?

**Feeny**  Will you have me?

**Arrah**  No.

**Feeny**  Then to the divil wid him, ye have spoken his doom.

*He raises the stone,* **Arrah** *flies at him; they struggle,* **Shaun**'*s arm is seen over the edge of the battlement; it seizes* **Feeny**'*s ankle, who utters a cry. As he is dragged to the edge of the precipice, he throws up his arms, and falls over with a cry.* **Shaun** *throws himself on the platform breathless. An alarm, drums, cries outside.* **Arrah** *throws herself on her knees beside* **Shaun**. *They embrace.*

*Enter the* **Sergeant**, *Soldiers with torches,* **O'Grady**, **Beamish**, **Fanny**, *the* **Major**, *omnes except* **Oiny**.

*An alarm without. Cries.* **Shaun** *leaps up and hides himself in a corner of the ruin.* **Arrah** *conceals him by standing before the nook in which he has taken refuge. Drums.*

*Enter Soldiers, with torches, the* **Major**.

**Major**  A man has fallen from the battlements into the lake below.

*Enter* **O'Grady**, *and the* **Sergeant**, *bearing* **Shaun**'s *clothes.*

**O'Grady**  It was Shaun. The poor fellow was trying to escape; he had broken through the bars of his prison window. We found the cell empty, and these clothes the evidence of his desperate adventure.

*Enter* **Fanny** *and* **Beamish**.

**Beamish**  He may be rescued yet. The boys had seen his attempt at evasion, and they put off in their boats to assist him if he fell.

**Fanny**  Heaven grant they may succeed!

**O'Grady**  A hundred pounds to the man that saves him! Ah! has he perished after all? It's a poor consolation for this unfortunate girl to know that here is Shaun's pardon. It has just come in time to be too late.

*Enter* **Oiny**.

**Oiny**  They've got him. I saw him pulled out of the wather lukin' like a dhrowned kitten.

**O'Grady**  Is he alive?

**Fanny**  It is impossible he can have survived a fall from so fearful a height.

**Shaun**  Spake up, ye thief, and tell me am I dead?

*Enter male and female Peasants, Soldiers, all mixed together, shouting, etc.*

**All**  Shaun!

**O'Grady**  Shaun himself!

**Beamish**  And alive?

**Fanny**  Oh, how glad I am to see you (*They bring him forward.*)

**Shaun**  You can't be gladder than I am to see myself.

**All**  Hurroo!

**Oiny**  Then who was it was washed up below there?

**Regan** (*entering*)   It was Feeny.

**O'Grady**   Feeny. I withdraw the reward.

**Major**   Feeny! What induced the fellow to commit suicide?

**Shaun**   I did, sir. He wanted me to go wid him, but I hadn't time, seein' I'm not half through my weddin' yet.

**Patsey** (*entering*)   He's recovered; but his washing is done for the rest of his life.

**O'Grady**   Hang him out to dhry.

**Beamish**   Shaun, can you forgive the sorrow I have caused you?

**Shaun**   Bless you for it, sir, for widout it I'd never have known how Arrah loved me. Ye think, maybe now, that she was in a bad way about you a while ago. But, oh, if you'd seen her afther me, I'd consint to be thried, convicted, and executed once a week to feel myself loved as I have been loved all this blessed day.

**Arrah**   Oh, I can hardly understand my sinses – it comes on me all of a suddint. Is there nothin' agin Shaun?

**Beamish**   Nothin, Arragh – he is free!

**All**   Hurroo!

**Arrah**   And he won't be tuk from me agin, will he, sir?

**O'Grady**   No – the law has no further call to him, nor to Beamish either; there is a free pardon to both.

**Arragh**   D'ye hear that, Shaun?

**Shaun**   I do, dear; but it's a mistake; it isn't a pardon I've got. Instead of death, I'm to be transported for life – and it's yourself that's to see the sintence rightly carried out, my darlin'.

**Arrah**   Ah, sure, I've done nothin' but what any woman in my place would have done. It is when a man is in throuble that

the breast of his girl grows bowld agin misfortune. When he's
wake, she's sthrong, and if he can purtect her wid his arm,
she can cover him wid her heart. It's then she is full of sinse
an' cuteness – for her heart gets into her head, and makes
a man of her entirely. It's to the famales of my own sex I
appale in this case. Had any of ye been in my place would
ye have done a ha'porth less for the man you loved than was
done by Arrah-na-Pogue?

*Curtain.*